LONG LANE
with *Turnings*

LONG LANE
with *Turnings*

L.J.K. SETRIGHT

Introduction by
Michael Bywater

Afterword by
James May

Granta Books
London

Granta Publications, 2/3 Hanover Yard, Noel Road, London
N1 8BE

First published in Great Britain by Granta Books 2006

A CIP catalogue record for this book is available from the
British Library.

1 3 5 7 9 10 8 6 4 2

ISBN-13: 978-1-86207-872-7
ISBN-10: 1-86207-872-6

Typeset by M Rules

Printed and bound in Great Britain by
William Clowes Limited, Beccles, Suffolk

INTRODUCTION

By Michael Bywater

There are many things for which Leonard Setright should be remembered: his informed (and rarer) instinctive understanding of engineering; his religious scholarship; his exquisite manners; his eclecticism of learning, worn lightly until challenged, and then wielded like a surgeon's blade, just enough and no more; his remarkable and sui generis appearance. All of these are revealed (though the Talmudic Setright perhaps less than the rest) in his writing about motor cars. As for that, *res*, as L. J. K. would have said, *ipse loquitur* (perhaps noting that *loquor* was of the class of verb known as a 'deponent'). As for the rest, as he might also have said, *de minimis non curat lector*.

But this modest prolegomenon to his last book demands that one writes *de minimis* and leaves the rest to his own words.

There can be few men who possessed (or possessed themselves of) such a remarkable physical presence. In appearance he resembled a gentlemanly instance of the Prophet Elijah; in demeanour, the manners and almost feline bearing of the kind of English gentleman otherwise long-since vanished. Yet a certain self-awareness – almost, but not quite, as if he were in on a small private joke with himself – marked the traces of his Antipodean forebears. Though he was a Londoner born and made, his parents were Australian: his father an engineer and his mother a fashion-buyer. Nobody whose veins were solely filled with pure English blood, six parts rainwater, could chain-smoke Sobranie Black Russian cigarettes through a long holder as if it were a perfectly simple trick; nor, indeed, carry off the great black fedora with quite such a combination of ease and panache.

The fedora carried a multiple narrative. It spoke, in its exoticism, of the Man from Elsewhere (and there can be few greater Elsewheres than the other side of the world), yet made subtle obeisance to the swooping outback Akubras of his parents' homeland, duly civilized, tamed, brushed and steamed. Simultaneously, it spoke of its own origins in the great omphalos of London elegance: Herbert Johnson's once majestic hat shop in New Bond Street. The particular model, being no mere fedora, but the Herbert Johnson flagship hat, 'The Poet', gave a well-fitted nod to his prose and to his sensibilities. And, finally, it also spoke eloquently of another side of L. J. K.'s life when, in 1980, he moved abruptly to America. There, in Texas, he fell in with a Lubavitcher group, and rediscovered not only his love for his motorbike (which he had shipped out and, of course, sharply tweaked) but also his Judaism, becoming, with his customary diligence and love of learning, a respected authority on matters of Jewish ritual, consulted and respected by *rebbeim* and scholars and writing regularly for the *Jewish Chronicle*, among others. In England, the Black Hat speaks, inter alia, of devout Judaism; but it was, of course, from Bond Street. (The last Lubavitcher rebbe, Menachem Mendel Schneerson, wore a hat L. J. K. would not have been seen in, alive or dead. And the hat Mr Setright brought back from Texas was, appropriately, the great American symbol of the elegant and self-determining traveller, the Royal Stetson 'Open Road'.)

Setright's writing told as many tales as Setright's black hat. He was the antithesis of the modern motoring writer who constructs, at best, workmanlike 'reader-benefit' reports, or, at worst, oafish, Mister Toad-ish blasts of vainglory and cheap testosterone. The idea of Sky Television's new motoring programme – no, *car* programme; motoring has little to do with it – being called *Vroom Vroom* would have confirmed all L. J. K.'s worst fears. His attention was all towards the motor car, and the motor car's life in society; his first touchstone was not what the car could do for him, but its engineering. He responded to fine, and above all elegant, engineering with an almost visceral sensuality (unsurprising in one who was also an accomplished musician) and to the motor car itself as the portal to freedom. And so it once was, just as smoking once was good for you: 'two of the greatest pleasures known to man,' as he described them in *Drive On!* (2003).

Perhaps this makes him seem like a man out of his

time; and, to some extent he was. The virtues extolled in Setright's writing (and indeed in his life) are not the qualities of modern – or postmodern – man. He liked to think, and to provoke thinking; he was devout; he moved happily among the classical authors and the great composers. He disapproved of the marketing culture, particularly as it applied to cars. But put him before fine engineering and he sung with pleasure. Here he is on the influence of motor racing on Mercedes-Benz's car design:

> There is more to progress than going faster or even stopping faster. The other half is more a matter of physical welfare than of sensual satisfaction, embracing matters of comfort, convenience, durability, economy and, in the most narrow-minded sense, respectability.
>
> Successfully to combine both these kinds of evolution, to satisfy at once the criteria both of the market place and of the race track, is to achieve a further degree of civilization of the car . . . Throughout the joint and several histories of Mercedes and Benz, there have been sports cars. The blend of track and town, iron fist and velvet glove has

not always been as smooth as might be hoped; there was too much sports in some of them, too much car in others. In turn the most brilliant and most baffling of them all, the most lumpen blend of *suaviter in modo and fortiter in re*, was the 300 SL . . .*

The measured tone, the moral admonition, the classical reference, the neatly turned aphorism:- all these are pure Setright, and a long way from the blaring of *Vroom Vroom*. And rightly so; the motor car has more radically changed our world than any amount of art or literature, so why should it not deserve – or indeed demand – the same degree of critical respect?

And from Setright, it gets it; not because he was a *car* enthusiast – he insisted that he was nothing of the sort – but because he was an *engineering* enthusiast, something he had perhaps learned literally at his father's knee at the engineering company which provided the family's substantial prosperity. The Rolls-Royce, the nurse, the expeditions: these were the predictable rewards of a suc-

---

* L. J. K. Setright, *Osprey Expert Histories: Mercedes-Benz SL & SLC* (Oxford: Osprey, 1979)

cessful engineer. The music, the elegance, the touch of the exquisite about L. J. K.: these were the rewards of the engineer's son. It is the standard British story: papa bashes metal so that the son can become a gentleman, with overtones (though inverted; the return was as respectable as the parents) of *Great Expectations*. After all, one didn't *come back* from Australia; one *went* there . . .

But the story was not at all like that. Leonard Setright inherited his music from his father's family, professors of music in Sydney from the mid-eighteenth century, and it was awakened by his father's violin: Kreisler party-pieces while little L. J. K. lay in his cot. (He may, too, have inherited his motoring instincts from his maternal grandfather, known for driving the fastest pony-cart in the area.) And far from turning away from the source of his family's prosperity, he writes lovingly of his father's 'exquisite precision work in light alloys'. The key word is 'exquisite', and it is typically Setright. Perhaps nobody explained to his father that here in England an engineer was unformed, stolid, rough, not to be associated with words like 'exquisite' . . . and as for playing the violin:

never. And so L. J. K. never learned that engineering was somehow *not*, my dear, part of *culture*.

Long Lane With Turnings is a fitting note for L. J. K. Setright to take his leave of us. When he was asked to write about motoring for *Punch* (under Alan Coren, the last great editor of that sadly fallen institution) he came to one of the celebrated Friday lunches, arriving far too early and taking root in the office of David Taylor, then deputy editor and himself an accomplished motoring writer. I was in Taylor's office at the time, and, delighted at Setright's appearance, settled back to watch him, but prepared – as a pilot, I had decided that I spurned cars and couldn't imagine how anyone could find them exciting – to be stupefied.

I was not. He sat on the edge of Taylor's desk and talked of his childhood; he talked of Texas. He spoke of training the reflexes, the responsibility of the individual, the different degrees of Latakia tobacco and the superiority of Yenidje; he discoursed upon *The Dream of Gerontius* and the impossibility of living by clarinet-playing, of the Philharmonia Chorus (of which he had been a co-founder) and the impossibility of the law (which he had studied) as a profession and of the joy of reviewing lorries (which I remember only hazily, and am delighted to see revisited here [p.115]) for *Machine Age*. He spoke of his beloved Bristol cars, of their engineering, and of engineering in general as though it were one of the great *litterae humaniores* of which most of us remain sadly ignorant, so missing one of life's tremendous joys, not just in the products that engineering gives to us, but in the thing itself (and, of course, he was quite right). And, eventually, as we filed into the dining room for our pre-luncheon drinks, he began upon the subject of ritual slaughter.

Setright writes as he spoke: terribly English, slightly mocking, sure of his judgements though kindly in condemnation where condemnation was called for; always with one eye alert for the interesting social detail – for example, his claim that motorists could at one stage go uninsured provided they deposited a £10,000 surety with the Bank of England – and the other for the chance to épater les bourgeois with his enthusiasm for speeding, his contempt for environmentalists, his mild sympathies with Mussolini.

It is tradition to say, when a man's last book is published posthumously, that we shall not see his like again. In this case it is true. Nobody – *Vroom Vroom!* – will write about the motorcar like L. J. K. Setright. Just a little further away than the eye can see – still a speck in the road, kicking up a train of dust – comes the time when nobody will drive motor cars like he, or any of us, have been so blithely driving for this brief and happy time in our history. To be reminded of it is a mitzvah, for sure.

1

FORMATIVE

Was it motoring, or was it music? Which came first? I shall never know – nor do I suppose that it should matter, provided that both endure as long as I do. Perhaps it might matter to a psychologist or some such investigative brain-picker; doubtless there are endless theories to be woven from an identification of somebody's earliest memory. It cannot be helped: I have two earliest memories, by which I mean that I am unable to deduce which came first.

In one of them, I am lying on my back in my cot and my father is standing alongside, playing his violin. I am not even sure what he was playing: it was perhaps *Caprice Viennoise Schöne Rosmarin*, one of those delicate, elegant party pieces by Fritz Kreisler that he played so often and so nicely. We all adored Kreisler in those days and Father was a good violinist, performing with that grace which seemed to me to pervade everything he did. He was competent at the keyboard too (we had a piano and a harmonium in the drawing room, both of them useful for our musical parties), and for some strange reason could also play the old English accordion, but the violin drew out his most expressive playing and clearly made a very early impression on me.

In the other of my memories struggling for priority, I am waking up on my nurse's lap in the back of a Rolls-Royce. Night has fallen, and beyond the buttoned leather upholstery of the car's rear compartment, beyond the glass division, I admire the soft violet lighting of the instruments on the dashboard. Father has dismounted to open the gates to our garage drive, and the engine is idling – not with a murmur, but with a faint rustle.

This was not, it must be admitted, a bad start to a motoring career. If you make your start, in any walk of life, somewhere near the top of the ladder, you may with fair ease proceed in either direction. If you start from the bottom it may be that there is nowhere to go but upwards, but it will be a long and laborious climb; the only easy choice at that stage is to get off, and go away to govern New South Wales or to be a writer or something similarly futile. For a motoring critic, the inside of a Rolls-Royce is a splendid vantage-point from which to begin – but at that tender age, barely a year, I did not know that it was a Rolls-Royce: I was merely an interested observer.

Not that I took any interest in the series of tall and terribly prim Austin 16hp saloons that Father subsequently used as 'business' cars. He did not keep the R-R long, and used to joke that it took half a gallon of petrol to start it, but I learned much later that what he actually disliked was the servo system operating the brakes. Decades later, I was to share his opinion.

In that decade, motoring was merely one of the countless phenomena that an infant has to interpret through such senses as seem relevant. To this day there are people who seem to be amused or appalled by the Setright nose (cartoonists and photographers especially), but they cannot know how important it was as an evaluation instrument in those early motoring experiences. Cars were rich in smells in those days: their upholstery, whether leather or some such substitute as Rexine, and regardless of whether the underlying cushioning were of horsehair or rubber (or even rubberised horsehair, as though to make doubly sure), always had a peculiarly industrial pong which grew stronger in warm weather, but even so it was only a background to the stronger odours of petrol, oil and exhaust smoke. Petrol tanks and carburettors were vented to the atmosphere, which meant that fuel vapours could get out as readily as air could get in. There were commonly leaks at every junction between those two termini (tank and carburettor), liquid and enduring when cold, vaporous and emetic when hot. The same sensitivity to temperature was displayed in the equally commonplace oil leaks from engines, gearboxes, back axles and anything else that had to be oiled rather than greased – though some of the greases that were then used freely on sundry suspension and steering joints developed a heavily tallow-tinged odour when hot. As for the smell of the exhaust fumes, dragged along behind or beside the car in its turbulent wake, it spoke volumes about the efficiency of combustion in the engine and the probability of distress in the stomach.

All this was evident even in an open car. In a saloon –

enclosed bodies had so many chinks and apertures in them that it was a gross inexactitude to describe them as 'closed' – a variable selection of all these several stinks was admitted, contained, stirred, and in summer heated, to enrich the interior atmosphere with a hydrocarbon cocktail that could sometimes overwhelm all the perfumes of Coty and the tobacco haze of De Reszke. Were it not for the disinclination of petrol vapour in air to ignite except within a surprisingly narrow range of mixture strengths, it might have been dangerously explosive to smoke in the car; fortunately, kindly Nature allowed it, and generous ashtrays were often to be found within saloon cars.

For me in my motoring infancy it might have been helpful if the interior equipment had included some sort of vomitorium. In those smelly circumstances, travel sickness was not unknown. The usual antidote was to open a window or two and blast a draught of fresh air through the interior, a procedure not unwelcome in summer but disturbing at other times. Welcome or not, it was sometimes essential in cold weather if we were to see out of windows that would otherwise have misted

Setright at the start.

faster than we could wipe them clear. Condensation on the inside of the glass was inevitable when interior heaters were unknown; on the outside it was fog, in which case one might at best open the windscreen, hinged at the bottom in the majority of open cars and at the top in saloons, so that one peered through the atmospheric fog rather than the stuff deposited on the glass.

What fogs they were! See them, smell them, taste them, feel them – they were thick and coloured and reinforced with the smoke that poured from every industrial and domestic chimney throughout the autumn and winter months that lasted so long when one had only a child's years against which to measure them. The basic tinge was the grey that must be common, I suppose, to all fogs, but the overtones of brown or green or sulphurous yellow varied, not only from place to place but even from hour to hour, in fogs that could last for days on end. As a five-year-old I would sometimes have to walk home from school more by feel and dead reckoning than by observation, so little was there to see. For motorists, few of whom enjoyed foglamps worthy of the description, and with dipping systems that often shut off one headlamp while dipping or even swivelling the other to the nearside, the problems of smoke-laden fog could often be countered only by the same techniques as were regularly adopted by the drivers of trams and buses: get somebody to walk in front carrying a torch. Not an electric torch – that would have been useless. A torch of more ancient prescription was needed, a hefty cone made up of sticks of wood and old sacking liberally tarred, flaming freely and making its own contribution to the smoke.

There was always smoke in the towns, even in midsummer. Though they could not compete with the coal fires of the colder months, cars and other vehicles made their own contributions to add to whatever any local factories discharged. Only the most modern of car engines had oil-control rings on their pistons, and none of them had oil-seals on their valve guides: lubricating oil slipped through both routes into the combustion chambers, and emerged from the exhaust pipe as a fine blue or a foul black smoke. Lorries were far worse, but the champion air-foulers were the steamers, whose output of smoke roared from their furnaces as untamed as the vapour from their boilers and valve-chests.

Like all little boys I used to gaze entranced at the steamrollers to be found smoothing the streets when road-surface repairs were being made; unlike most of the others, since I was the studious son of parents who loved modernity, I was developing some understanding of the internal combustion engine but had not a clue about, nor much interest in, steam engines. What fascinated me was the sheer size and ponderous motion of these behemoths, not to mention the obviously vague steering control which required so much twirling of the wheel to accomplish so very little deviation, compared with the prompt response to the wheel evident in proper motor cars.

Steamrollers were merely entertainment. Steam wagons were a different matter. When coal was what heated every house most of the colliery companies used to deliver it in large jute sacks borne on horse-drawn wagons, from which it would be carried to each home by big burly blackened men in filthy but durable clothes and wearing black leather hats with vast tailpieces which hung down over the shoulders and back. However, a couple of local colliers employed steam tractors, by Foden or by Sentinel, to haul their wagons. While the team of horses stood still and quiet to rest during a delivery the fire had to keep going, and a glimpse into the inferno when a stoker opened the furnace door to shovel some more coal into that hell-sent contraption was enough to frighten me stiff. I never lingered long in my awestruck contemplation of either of these steamers: if the fire did not leap out and get me, Satan probably would.

Smoke from coal or oil was always rather deplorable, an admission that we had not yet found an efficient way to fuel our lives. Tobacco smoke was an entirely different affair in an era when people smoked more – more generally, more assiduously, more desperately – than ever before or since. My senses were attuned to the fragrance of the Turkish tobacco in the De Reszke cigarettes that my father smoked (they came in handsome enamelled tins of twenty or fifty; almost everything small could be bought in tins then, from biscuits to steel gramophone needles), and some pipe-smokers generated wonderful scent-clouds of Burley, Yenidje or whatever. Some of my parents' friends did even better, most memorably the one who flaunted an amazingly elegant Egyptian cigarette tipped with rose-petals. Alas, *hoi polloi* smoked cheap Virginia or even more rank 'Empire' (that is, Rhodesian) blends of acrid stench. I could tolerate this, even feel comforted by it, in such concentrations as I encountered in cinemas (yes, everybody smoked in there, too – England was once an impressively free country), but in the upper compartment of a bus or tram the smoke seemed almost solid, and the young Setright tum could not manage a lengthy journey without feeling queasy.

Going motoring with Father was nicer in every way. There was no question of this during the working week, nor I think on Saturdays (though ours was not a religiously observant household), but on a fine Sunday we loved to go for a run in the car out into the country. Sometimes it would only be to Epping Forest, with perhaps a foray to North Weald Basset where we could watch the RAF flying, but our favourite jaunts were into Buckinghamshire.

We liked it so much that, for a couple of summers in

Setright with his parents, summer 1933.

the late 1930s, we rented a house there for the holidays. It was on the edge of Stoke Mandeville, then a mere village, and I was intrigued again by the business of delivering domestic goods. Milk came in aluminium churns on a pony cart, from which the churn was carried to our door along with a couple of cylindrical measuring jugs (long-handled and again of aluminium) with which the desired quarts or pints might be ladled into such receptacles as we had to hand. The milkman, Duggie (Douglas) Wakefield, once offered me a ride in his pony-cart up the road and back, and from the high vantage point of the cart, at the modest speed of a quadruped trot, I took my first interest in the road surface over which our car had rolled in such obliterating comfort. I noted the roundness of the crown of the road, and how the passage of such traffic as it suffered sent all the loose fine gravel down to the sides, and how the edges were bounded not by kerbstones but by grass, even though this was the main road to Aylesbury.

By that time we were enjoying something better than those dismally self-righteous Austins. In 1936 Father fell for the new Wolseley Super Six, and bought the 2-litre

16hp version. It was architecturally similar to the coeval
Morris, in effect a sensibly British expression of what was
best about modern American saloons: easy-clean pressed-
steel wheels, tyres of generous proportions by the
standards of the times, an in-line six-cylinder engine (with
overhead valves, which was more than most Americans
could claim) located further forward for the sake of ride
comfort as well as of interior space, a synchromesh gearbox, and such modern features as an electrical fuel pump,
not to mention generally modern styling. A business part-
ner had bought the 25hp Morris, but father's Wolseley
outsmarted it in everything but power: the gearbox had
four speeds rather than three, there was a proper extended
luggage boot, and the trim and furnishings were altogether
more luxurious. There was even an illuminated Wolseley
badge on the front of the radiator grille, but the refinement
which most impressed me (in those days when punctures
were not only a perpetual hazard but also a frequent
occurrence, and wheel-changing therefore a regular chore)
was the built-in jacking system.

Pushing the driver's seat fully to the rear revealed a
panel set into the floor. Raising that disclosed an

hydraulic pump with a socket for a tubular aluminium handle which could be inserted into the socket on the pump. There was also a switch to select front or rear jacking. Waggling the handle forwards and backwards pumped hydraulic fluid to a pair of hydraulic jacks on the selected axle, and they responded by extending downwards until they reached the road and started lifting the car. To reverse the procedure, opening a bleed valve adjacent to the pump allowed the weight of the car to telescope the jacks, after which a few strokes on the lever completed their retraction. It was all remarkably easy, and far more civilized than messing about with old-fashioned screwjacks. I did hear allegations of these jacks letting themselves down on to the road while the car was in motion, but ours never gave any trouble.

Father really liked his Wolseley and never contemplated replacing it, even when that model was replaced after a couple of years by one with a more bulbous body – the one which was taken up by the Metropolitan and other police forces, their first Wolseley and the start of a long police association with the brand. However, he did from time to time contemplate buying an extra car, a small one to serve as a runabout for my mother – she did not drive, but the factory driver could often be spared from his primary duties – and thus I garnered some experience in a variety of little machines that I thought quite appalling. There was a Singer 8hp saloon, for example, that stayed with us only two days before rejection as inadequate even for a hencoop, and a rather more roomy Humber tourer painted in a flat dull fudge brown that seemed to be a Humber speciality. All I noticed in the latter was the use of a rounded trim-strip (it was a rolled aluminium section, I think) screwed on to the timber framework to cover the top edges of the open body; that car was as flat and dull as it was painted.

None of these experiments came to anything. I dare say Mother did not enter into the spirit of them, not when one of the more dashing of her smart friends drove herself around in a 25hp Opel cabriolet, quite lightly constructed and accordingly lively. Instead we saw much more of the Wolseley at home than we ever did of its predecessors. It was also called upon for lengthy business trips, especially to Scotland where Father had strong connections with John Sword, a great motoring enthusiast and notable collector. Mother sometimes accompanied him (I recall she went with him to Glasgow for the Empire Exhibition in 1938) and on one such trip they called for some reason upon George Brough, the proprietor of Brough Superior, who tried unsuccessfully to sell Father one of his new and very handsome (and very accelerative) cars.

At that time Brough's Nottingham factory was doubtless being gathered into the Ministerial network of outside suppliers to the aircraft industry, as part of the rearmament drive which began in May 1935. Father's Walthamstow factory, doing exquisite precision work in light alloys, was likewise on the war-work schedule, so perhaps the two men had interests in common. George Brough, however, was no engineer; he was a good and brave motorcyclist, and a brilliant salesman. His motorcycles were really assembly jobs, employing superior components from the best suppliers and with great attention paid to fit and finish. Many years later I had occasion to write some criticism of them, and soon had a letter from some reader who was a BS enthusiast and, reprimanding me for my impertinence, observed that his 'father had the honour to know George Brough'. I could not believe that someone should so fail to honour a parent, and wrote back pointing out that George Brough had the honour to know my father.

The comfortable Wolseley would have made a decent job of such journeys. It was good for 82mph and cruised easily in the fifties, which was more than the maximum speed of many of the cars then on the roads of Britain. Our familial Sunday jaunts were nevertheless always leisurely, though I would often stand behind Father's seat and exhort him to 'go fast!'. Reason told me that to travel more slowly than one could was a waste of time and opportunities, but Father (perhaps rightly, noting that what I had demanded was not merely the comparative 'faster' but unmistakably the absolute 'fast') took no notice.

Fast drivers were rare then, but I recall a day when, as I stood idly on the pavement opposite our uniquely modern house at the end of a very wide and very long avenue of magnificent Edwardian and Victorian villas, somebody came rushing past, driving a Hillman Minx as hard as it would go. Then, in urgent pursuit, came a police Wolseley – and the thing that I noticed particularly was that neither car made a suitable engine noise to match its speed. Instead, the exhaust pipe of each emitted a loud hiss, and I observed that both exhaust pipes were of small diameter. Thus began a childish evaluation of gas dynamics from which, for many years, I reasoned that exhaust tailpipe diameter must eventually determine maximum power because, no matter how large the engine, the size of the exit aperture must limit the throughput of combustible mixture. It was an oversimplification, but it was a start.

The outbreak of war in 1939 put a stop to all that, as to much else. Blackout regulations were imposed: streetlights (apart from those on main roads, most of them were gas-fired, being ignited and doused at dusk and dawn by a man carrying a long pole on a bicycle) were extinguished, windows of all buildings were heavily curtained or shuttered. Vehicle headlamps had to be masked, and at one stage only one masked light was allowed: the effect was to cause more vehicle accidents than at any other time, more injuries and fatalities than the air raids that the blackout was meant to forestall. In the first two years of the war there were more people killed on our roads than in our armed services.

This was a remarkable result, considering how little traffic there was. Petrol rationing, continuing throughout the war and for some time after it, had strangled it. Tyres were almost unobtainable, which made matters worse. The petrol rationing inevitably generated a black market, as did the rationing of other commodities including many food items: this situation provided endless fascinating exercises in morality and ethics, with what appeared criminal in some circumstances taking on the air of a workers' cooperative in others.

One did a lot of walking, and a lot more standing in queues. We queued for almost everything, and we all did it very well, very nicely and responsibly and politely. Journeys that defied walking could only be made if there were a convenient bus service, but the buses were infrequent and overloaded so one had to queue for those too, and it sometimes took a lot of standing in the cold and wet and wind before one gained access to one of those snug and stuffy interiors. Upstairs (I thought in those days that all buses were double-deckers) everybody smoked; downstairs it was forbidden, but standing passengers were allowed there when all the seats were full (I suppose it helped to keep the centre of mass low), and the conductor who struggled to get through the crammed interior and take fares found it particularly easy to pocket some of the takings. This being London, the conductors used Bell punches to perforate the coded edge of a pre-printed ticket, and few passengers bothered to inspect theirs, even fewer knowing what the code represented. No doubt it was different in the country, for many country bus services (and, I think, all those in Scotland, thanks to Father's connections up there with the likes of John Sword) issued their conductors with Setright Registers, beautiful little ticket-printing machines of Duralumin and enamel which had an air of camera technology about them and were designed to be proof against conductors' cupidity.

The Setright Registers factory in Walthamstow was bombed during the winter Blitz of 1940-1941, but it was engaged in work for the MoAP and that work had to continue. When I was taken to see it after the initial repairs and tidying, all I remember was a huge hole where most of a wall had been demolished by the bomb and a big coke brazier of sheet metal erected in the

The Athletics squad. William Ellis School,
London 1943/4. Setright centre back.

middle of the machine-shop floor to keep the poor machinists warm in that bitter weather. The fumes from the coke seared the lungs; a year later my father was dead. Almost simultaneously my brother was invalided out of the Royal Air Force after flying with Bomber Command (mostly in Blenheims and Whitleys) and being landed on occasions by pilots experiencing various difficulties. In the early days of flying they used to say that a good landing was one from which you could walk away, but I doubt if he would agree.

So at the age of ten I still had a senior man at home, not exactly *in loco parentis* but at least providing me with some sort of role model. Many other lads of my age had no men at home during the war or, in some cases, after it. My brother was very good to me, as he has always been, but inevitably I was left to do much of my own thinking and to manage my own life so far as my mother allowed. What pained and puzzled me was that she imposed a regimen of stringent economies after Father died, as though we had been left poor (it was many years before I learned that we had not), so there was not much organizing for me to do.

What made this hurt even more was that it was preceded by a very pleasant interlude of six months during which, my mother being in hospital recovering from the enormous strain of Father's last dying months, I went to stay with the family of one of his business partners, in a pleasant Edwardian villa in Barnet. It was a polite and serene household, enlivened weekly by the youngest son (in his late teens) bringing home one of the latest Artie Shaw records to reach these shores. Thus, if Father's life had inculcated in me a love of music, it was his death which occasioned that love being focused upon the clarinet.

Four more years were to elapse before I acquired one and found in it a transport of delight. Meanwhile, some form of more literal and practical transport became desirable; I could walk forever and run pretty well, but the distances I wanted to cover demanded more speed. Even so, this progression to wheels was very nearly postponed by another of my enthusiasms, which was for guns.

Setright in the spirit of the times, 1937.

When it started I have no idea, but by this time I was already accustomed to seeing shooting tools of some sort around the house – or, more practically, in the rear garden. Father had been a naturally good shot, even though he preferred fishing (and, I hardly need add, was very good at it); my brother, in inexplicable contrast, was an unnaturally good shot, in particular spectacularly effective when shooting with sporting rifle or pistol at aerial targets ranging in size from mallard to halfpennies. We did a lot of plinking in the garden, and whatever his weapon I had no hesitation in holding up a small card target for him. We also went shooting grey squirrels and woodpigeon in the local park, the Town Hall issuing a permit for this to be done in the early hours of Sunday mornings as part of the war effort. The park's grounds had been largely given over to allotments serving the 'Dig for Victory!' campaign, and those creatures had been identified as vermin because of their depredations upon the harvests.

Sometimes we went with a family living nearby who had remarkable shooting credentials. The father, then over seventy years of age, had in the past captained a British Olympic shooting team, as had his wife, twenty years his junior. The old man had been a traveller for Remington, and apparently never went out without a gun in some pocket of every garment – waistcoat, trousers, jacket and overcoat. The mother used to bicycle around in the countryside with a double-barrelled .410 shot-pistol in the basket on her handlebars, and if any rabbit of cookworthy size caught her eye it was dead before her cycle had come to a halt. In the park on Sunday mornings they would lend me a shotgun, usually either a modern lightweight short-barrelled 12-bore of the kind that the gunmaker Churchill favoured in the 1930s or else an elderly and exquisite 20-bore with external hammers and Damascus barrels.

The upshot of all this was that, as my twelfth birthday approached my mother, in a fit of unfamiliar generosity, offered me as a present for the occasion my choice between a 12-bore shotgun and a bicycle – both second-hand, inevitably, and presumably found by my brother acting as her scout. I did not long hesitate:

dreamer I might have been, but severe practical need dictated my answer for me, and I opted for the bicycle. This just goes to show what a simple innocent I have always been: only years later did it occur to me that I should have taken the gun and then shot the chap who had the bicycle.

A very fine bicycle it was, by the standards of the time – the sort of machine one might see being pedalled very steadily and assiduously by robust-looking men wearing plus fours and determined expressions. Not quite a racing bike but a very sporting tourer, it was a late pre-war New Hudson of light weight and elaborate specification. At a time when fashionable riders chanted mantras about Reynolds' 431 tubing, which was of a nickel-chrome steel alloy, mine had a frame composed of Accles & Pollock tubes toughened by a further measure of vanadium. It also had a close-ratio Sturmey-Archer three-speed hub which I have never seen elsewhere and was a joy to use. Derailleur gears were troublesome in those days and not much favoured, the rare exception being the now forgotten Cos gear, a mere two-speeder with its selector arm arcing down below the bottom bracket.

The pedal bicycle is a noble instrument, and I have always enjoyed studying the detail felicities which illustrate its development. Even today, the failure of designers to recognize and reject the shortcomings of the original basic layout and frame design is a continuing intellectual offence – but such little lightweight felicities as centre-pull caliper brakes, quick-release hubs, rat-trap pedals with skeleton toe-clips and quick-buckled straps, alloy-framed saddles, and so on, could and did in those days enchant me as readily as most niceties of mechanical engineering; yet the thing to which I was really sensitive was the fiability of the steering, and the geometry of my New Hudson frame seemed perfect.

What bliss it was in that dawn to be riding – and to be riding a really good bicycle was very heaven. The roads were empty, the countryside only a few miles distant, and even the suburban streets constituted challenges to one's concern for taking a good speed-sustaining line through corners. I rode hard and long, and always as fast as I could. In winter when darkness

came all too early, lighting was demanded, but I took a
dim view of the dim glimmer of electric lamps powered
by battery or dynamo. Instead I took pride in an old
Lucas acetylene lamp, mounted on parallel links sprung
to cushion the road's jolts. It was charged with water
and lumps of calcium carbide, and when the valve was
opened to allow the former to drip upon the latter
there was generated not only a most unusual (but not
actually unpleasant – not quite) smell but also acetylene gas. Lighting the two convergent jets with a match
produced a brilliant flame which, with a generous
reflector behind and a big bullseye lens in front, created
a mildly divergent light beam that by bicycle standards
was quite respectable.

The birthday which ushered me into a new revelation of mobility occurred in August 1943. Within a
year I found myself in a quandary about another great
and long-entrenched enthusiasm, which was for aircraft. I propose to write more about this later in this
book, but the problem in the autumn of 1944 was that
there were suddenly relatively few aircraft to be seen.
There had been spectacular air battles to watch from

the garden during the Battle of Britain in 1940: I remember especially the momentous affair of 15 September, with fighters glinting brilliantly as the sun caught them in a roll or dive. There had been stupendous air raids during the nights of the two ensuing winters: again I remember one in particular, the clear night sky full of flashes from bombs and anti-aircraft guns, and the brilliantly silvery trace of phosphorus, dropped from a bomber crossing my line of vision, shining with nothing less than vehemence and skidding horizontally for some distance when it met a sudden atmospheric change – it must have put the bombardier's aim off considerably, if indeed phosphorus could be aimed. Later there were always hit-and-run raiders at low altitude, or massed fleets of American heavy bombers filling the morning sky with condensation trails as they headed for Germany – we never saw their rags-and-tatters return after dusk. By the summer of 1944, however, about the only things we saw flying were V1 doodlebugs, sounding like basso profundo two-strokes and going like stink. We heard that Hawker Tempests, exploiting their prodigiously powerful

Napier Sabre engines, were catching many of them (nothing else was fast enough to catch a V1 in straight and level flight) off the south coast, but that was akin to retail business and the Hun was delivering the things in wholesale quantities.

As for all the other proper aircraft, they were now busy on the other side of the Channel. It was also clear from my unremitting study of aviation magazines that aircraft were becoming bigger and more complex, as well as more remote. What could I do to satisfy my desire to understand and be familiar with some still-developing form of powered mechanical transport? I made a conscious decision: I should have to revive my dormant interest in cars, which after all were still to be seen and after the war would presumably revive and flourish all around me.

So it proved. My reading pattern changed. There were hours of homework to be done after each school day, and I was engaged with my clarinet for hours more, but I still found hours to spend in the public library, devouring everything relevant as well as much that was not but which begged to be read. I went on like that for years, but once the war was over there began to be practical experience and enjoyment as well.

Mother decided to buy a car. My brother could drive her and at other times use it for his own purposes. When I went along, I watched and mentally measured his every movement, calculated the mutual responses of car and driver, assessed the effects of wind and rain and road surfaces, noted how the exploitation of road camber and the effect of speed dictated a different cornering line from what I had by now more or less perfected on two wheels. I compared all this with the behaviour of other cars and other drivers. I fixed in my memory the motions and commotions which occurred (and the action taken to correct them) whenever we had a puncture, which was all too often on those poor old tyres and those uncultivated roads. I worked out where one should be looking, and what to deduce from what one saw. I was learning to drive long before I was allowed to drive.

The car was a 1936 Morris 8 – not, thank goodness,

the horrid saloon which always reminded me of that
ghastly Singer though it was more strictly modelled on
Ford's disgusting Model Y of 1933, but the open four-
seater tourer. A two-seater Morris had been the first
£100 car on the British market, back in 1933 when the
Ford was new (Ford reduced their price to match in
1935), but the four-seat version made much more sense –
despite which my mother's doctor had one of each.

There was not much of it: the wheelbase was only
ninety inches and the track precisely half of that, with
a little cast-iron side-valve engine of 918cm^2 cowering
in the depths beneath the snubby bonnet. Yet there was
room for two tall young men (I was already well over
six feet) in the front seats with a decidedly adult lady of
medium height astern – or if she chose to sit with the
driver, I could sit behind her. All this was made possible by thinly padded upholstery, by the long-established
assumption that people should sit shoulder to shoulder
like the boys of the Old Brigade rather than demanding
elbow room, and by the readiness of designers to locate
the rear bench seat over the back axle to ensure adequate legroom. Cramped though they looked, many

old cars felt surprisingly roomy – and had to be to allow for the heavy and bulky clothing we wore in cold weather.

In such conditions the canvas hood could be erected without much effort, and celluloid side-screens framed in canvas-covered metal were plugged into sockets on the top edges of the two doors and the body flanks aft of them. All-around vision took a serious beating when this was deployed, and we often preferred to do without it if the weather were dry. On warm sunny days, especially if Mother were not aboard, the drill was to fold the windscreen flat (easily managed with a wing nut at each side) and enjoy the 360° vision which makes such a difference to the pleasure, as well as to the safety, of motoring.

Our enjoyment of it all was, if intense, at best sporadic. Petrol rationing continued after the war, and at one stage there was simply none of the stuff at all. From time to time, therefore, the car was laid up – as was the usual drill for many people who only drove in the summer months and laid their cars up for the winter. It was not just a matter of abandoning the poor thing in the garage – that is very bad for any motor car. It was jacked up and then lowered on to wood blocks (readily available in standard sizes in the old days) beneath the axles, so that the tyres were unloaded; the cooling system was drained (some people foolishly did this every night when they were using their cars in winter, despite the availability of anti-freeze which would protect the coolant during the day as well); and any rust-prone surfaces were treated with grease, oil, or whatever seemed appropriate.

Here was an opportunity for me to go through the motions of driving even if I was too young to be allowed on the road. Sitting in the car on its blocks, I could turn the steering and move the gear lever around, as well as work all the pedals. I mentally envisioned all kinds of driving circumstances, from starting to emergency stopping. I would go on my mental way, accelerating and steering and signalling and braking on routes that I had in my head, and all the time becoming entirely familiar with the location, the travel, and the feel, of the controls. Double-clutched downshifts through the three-speed gearbox became as mellifluous as snap upward changes, the motions of my hands on the steering wheel were trained to be smooth rather than jerky, my feet progressive on the pedals rather than sudden in their pressure. From what I had read about competition driving, I even made mental attacks on Shelsley Walsh hill-climb or some racing circuit, leaning into the corner as would be appropriate to counter the centrifugal force to be experienced. What I had in the garage was the best imaginable driving simulator, and I made the best possible use of it.

When the car was running I would use the garage drive for practising clutch engagement and the synchronization of that with handbrake release. Then on a sunny day in 1948 came the time when, aged seventeen, I could venture on to the public highway. The car was parked facing down the hill on which we lived. I settled into the driver's seat, my brother sat alongside and told me to start the engine, and then he issued his instructions: I was to start down the hill, shift from bottom gear directly into top, and take the second turning on the right. I managed all this decently, with a nice downshift into second gear for the corner . . .

The Setright Ticket Machine, in use
on buses for sixty years c. 1930–1990.

And that was that. Satisfied that I knew what I was doing and how to do it properly, my brother realized that all my future 'driving lessons' would really be experience sessions, and very rarely offered criticism or advice. It followed that when he did volunteer some comment, I took more notice than if he had been a constant niggler. Thus it was not long before I presented myself for the Dreaded Driving Test – something of which he had no experience, having obtained his driving licence (as was possible in certain pre-war circumstances) by simply going into a Post Office and buying it.

An exeat from school was necessary for me to keep my afternoon appointment with the driving examiner, but that was easy: I was in the Upper Sixth and could afford to miss a session on the second Punic War or Balzac's *Comédie Humaine* or whatever was involved. The test proceeded smoothly until, during a halt, the examiner explained that at some stage he would demand an emergency stop by shouting 'Stop!' and at the same time striking the windscreen with his folded newspaper. I knew that he would not do it if other vehicles were close behind, so if I used my mirror properly I would have at least some idea of when it might happen; and when I saw him begin to fold or roll his newspaper and snatch a glance behind (I am blessed with very good lateral vision) I had the brake pedal covered with my foot before he could shout his instruction. A little later that afternoon I proudly resumed my place in school, a licensed driver.

The Morris was not fast: down a long and straight and pretty steep hill I once managed an indicated 52mph in it, correcting with the aid of blessedly high-geared steering the jittery changes of direction it made with every bump or ridge. Being small and compact it was reasonably agile, however, and had quite decent hydraulic brakes, and I learned a lot about how to conserve momentum – learned, in effect, that high average speeds were not the result of going fast but of not going slowly.

The most interesting aspect of this car's behaviour was how, despite a good deal of roll steer in ordinary circumstances, its handling became very well balanced indeed on slippery surfaces. When the friction between tyres and road is slight there can be no very high lateral accelerations generated; there is therefore little or no lateral sway when cornering, and so the basic steering and suspension geometries remain uncorrupted. With all its masses contained within the wheelbase, and with very quick steering responses (as in many a vintage racer, going from lock to lock took only about one and a half turns of the wheel), the little Morris could be tossed around with alacrity and accuracy on skiddy surfaces.

That may be why I best remember it for a drive from Hereford to North London on New Year's Day 1951. We were three sizeable men in the car, all dressed up in heavy coats and scarves and warm gloves and head-gear, with the hood and screens down for the sake of visibility through the constantly falling snow. In the Vale of Evesham there was a downright blizzard, and everywhere it was bad – after leaving Hereford I did not actually see the road surface beneath the ice and snow until passing Northolt aerodrome. I did not see much traffic either, and comfortably overtook what-ever was going my way, but there were a lot of cars dumped unceremoniously on the verges of one long uphill stretch, their drivers having run out of resources. The Morris sailed up the middle between them all – but not straight up the middle: I was steering a serpentine course to reduce the effective gradient (a trick I taught myself when cycling) and thus improve the car's traction.

The Morris 8 may not have been a good car, it may even have been a loathsome car, but I was happy to accept it as it was and to make the best of it. I was rather more critical of what came next, if only because I paid for it with my own money. By this time I was doing my National Service in the Royal Air Force and was stationed at Sopley, a few miles inland from Bournemouth. There, deep in the countryside, was a large rotating aerial array: a Type 7 radar, affording a good three-dimensional view over the Channel and most of the southern counties. Underground was a cavernous operations room featuring large maps (one horizontal, one vertical) attended by a crew of plotters armed with headphones and long sticks, while surrounding offices were packed with radar screens. This was Southern Sector

Ground Control, from which we ordered and controlled fighter interceptions of all potentially hostile aircraft flying in our zone.

The life was, if decently dutiful, seldom exciting or entertaining, but there were odd occasions for diversion. One was when I had the task of landing a Meteor NF11 in the middle of the night by telephone, because his radio had frozen and he could not switch to his local (Tangmere, I think) frequency. Just before he ran out of fuel I got him down, with a last-second panic because there was another aircraft parked at the end of the runway. On another occasion, a fine sunny afternoon, we were controlling a pair of DH Vampires from Odiham doing practice interceptions when the prototype DH Comet airliner came into view, so we asked the pilot whether he would mind if we guided the Vampires on to him for practice. He replied with an amused affirmative, and so we set our fighters up to swing on to his tail in feigned attack. He did nothing until they were almost in position, then rammed his throttles wide open and simply shot away from them. Their howls of dismay were pitiful, for the fighters could not match his speed – a fine comment either on the first-line defences of our country or on the prowess of the world's first jet airliner.

RAF Sopley was, as I have noted, deep in the countryside. Thus there were occasions – not many, for I enjoyed being in the service – when I needed transport to take me elsewhere. In due course I found what every young man should experience early in his motoring career; a Morgan three-wheeler. It was the Aero model, dating from 1926, with a two-speed transmission involving chains for the final drive, one on each flank of the rear wheel. The engine was a v-twin JAP, albeit only the soft-tuned water-cooled side-valve job rather than the hot overhead-valve versions sometimes fitted. The body had been modified (sensibly, but not prettily) around the tail by a previous owner, who had also had the wit to scrap the hand-lever throttle control clamped to a steering-wheel spoke and substitute an accelerator pedal such as is familiar in cars.

More to the point, much of the machinery was worn out, but since I had only paid £57 10s Od for the thing I could not really complain. What had suffered worst was the carburettor, a handsome old brass Brown & Barlow instrument whose needle and surrounding jet had been so abraded by the passing of time and of each other that the delivery of mixture to the engine was decidedly imprecise. There was also dermatitis in the magneto, which made starting doubly problematic: sometimes it was instant, but I can recall occasions when I had to crank the blasted thing for nearly a quarter of an hour before it condescended to fire. In due course a new Amal carburettor (with which petrol consumption improved by 85 per cent) and a magneto rebuild cured these troubles, and that little Moggie gave me enormous satisfaction.

It was very strictly an open two-seater, almost a one-and-a-half-seater in the style of those racing cars which had been its contemporaries: the seats were staggered, the passenger's being slightly further back than the driver's. This reduced frontal area put the driver nearer the centre-line of the car the better to see and to steer. The passenger could also put his right arm behind the driver's shoulders to free more space and, if he could find something to grip, help him to stay in place when cornering, which the low and light Morgan did rather well.

Too well for its own good, perhaps. The front wheel hubs were more like those of a perambulator, or perhaps of a bicycle, than those of a car: with inadequate lateral bracing from the spokes they flexed inordinately, adding their own slip angle to that of the tyres so that the three-wheeler was unexpectedly a natural understeerer. After a couple of weeks of blissful three-wheel drifts along cursive lanes, spokes began to break. On one afternoon of strong sun, during which the Morgan was parked on a steeply cambered road, several spokes broke in one of the front wheels. On another occasion, as I took a 90-degree left-hander in the grounds of RAF Stanmore flat-out in the 36mph bottom gear, the offside wheel simply collapsed, and the Moggie finally grounded itself to a halt on the grass just a few feet from the building which, I learned, housed the RAF Theatrical Wardrobe. I still wonder why the service should need such a thing.

When the tiny chassis and running gear of the Morgan held together, it was a pleasure to be driving it. There is something so intrinsically right about a tricycle properly planned – the most vital criterion being that the centre of mass should be as low as feasible. That was certainly true of the low-slung Moggie: when I first took my brother out for a drive he shook his pipe out over the side prior to recharging it with tobacco, felt a slight jar, and brought his hand back holding merely the stem, for the bowl had hit the road and shattered!

The Morgan was not to be criticized for this, but rather the design of tobacco pipes. The low-slung design of the vehicle did more than merely make it stable: it enhanced the balance, because the tricycle has its rear roll centre more or less inevitably at road level beneath the rear tyre, so it is doubly desirable to keep the roll couple to a minimum by having a low centre of mass. In the Morgan front suspension layout, based on a sliding-pillar system that goes back before the original Moggie of 1909 to a pioneering Sizaire-Naudin, the instantaneous front roll centre is also at ground level; given stiff springing so that wheel travel is not excessive, the distance between roll axis and centre of mass stays reasonably constant, and so accordingly does the steering balance. Steering response was enhanced by the fact (seldom appreciated) that suspension of this kind provokes an anti-Ackermann toe-in when the vehicle rolls, so altogether (further enhanced by the correct distribution of masses in the horizontal plane) the nature of the vehicle was to be at once stable and responsive. Here was a fine example of a rare thing among motor vehicles but a natural one in tricycles: whatever the designer does that is good in one respect turns out to be good in others too.

All this promoted a good deal of confidence in driving, so that I could relax on almost any journey and enjoy the physical sensations to which a low, open, lightweight vehicle brings one so close. The surprisingly gentle pobble of the engine out in the open air ahead of the radiator was a steady reassurance; the smell of hot oil weeping from the valve guides, of fresh oil and petrol from the ventilated filler-caps ahead of me on top of the bonnet, were somehow confirmatory that all was working as it should, and were a mere scent carried away by the headwind, not a stink stuck in the cockpit. In the long dips and swells of the A30's

Making music in the RAF. Setright on clarinet.

gradients on a deep winter's night I could sense in my face the changes in air temperature and calculate whether the road surface was likely to be icy or dry; the rest of me was warmed by the air which blew in through the radiator and, heated there, continued into the cockpit to take the chill off the nether Setright. Motoring in open cars really does have a charm all its own, if one is not going too fast.

Nothing in those days was all that fast, and many of the cars I drove were pretty paralytic. The Morris had gone, and my brother had found a 1927 Lea-Francis tourer, the 1½-litre Meadows-engined 12/22hp model. The long open body was roomy and comfortable after the manner of its times, but the low-powered engine, the heavy flywheel and the wide-ratio gearbox all combined with typically weighty British build to rob the car of any pretensions to performance that the near-relation of a TT winner might have had. I could make far better progress on his motorcycle, a 1921 Triumph model H. Essentially a touring side-valver, it still invited one to exploit all the advantages that a two-wheeler enjoyed in those days: the ability to infiltrate traffic, to straighten corners, to respond promptly to circumstances.

We often found ourselves the brief tenants of other cars, lent for a quarter of an hour or a couple of days. Friends of mine had a vintage Riley Nine Monaco saloon, the one with a fabric body, and it impressed me by feeling lively and having a pleasant gearbox (especially when making clutchless shifts), although in fact it was another sluggard. A fascinating contrast was afforded by a Lancia Augusta of about the same size: the stiffer and more stable chassis, the powerful brakes, and an even nicer gearbox, made it actually quicker on the road than the older Riley despite a lower top speed.

Probably the slowest of them all was nearly new – a Bond three-wheeler. This was a very light tricycle indeed, and economically laid out with a single front wheel powered by a tiddly Villiers two-stroke attached so that it turned with the steering. Because the whole thing weighed next to nothing it stopped very well, but it could not go fast enough to demonstrate the dynamic hazards of its layout. In principle such a tricycle is only stable when driven backwards – but, because of the

British taxation regulations, a tricycle could only profit from the tax concessions offered to motorcycle/sidecar combinations if it weighed less than 5 cwt (a quarter of a ton) and had no reverse gear. Driving backwards was not on the cards.

In the Morgan a smart about-face could be accomplished by doing what would normally be a handbrake turn in most cars but in this case involved the footbrake, which acted only upon the rear wheel while the handbrake was coupled to the front drums. In the case of the Bond, if one could not turn the steering enough to make the front wheel point backwards, which should have been possible, one simply got out and lifted the tail of the car, swivelled the whole thing round, and put it down again. There is so much to be said for lightweight construction!

There is also much to be said in favour of having enough power to ensure high performance. In this sense, probably the high spot of this period was a vintage Bentley which my brother brought home in the hope that Mother would agree to its purchase. It was one of the rarest models, the Green Label 3-litre, with an extra-short wheelbase and the A-type Bentley gearbox which had internal ratios as close as any Bentley ever. The engine had been tuned and the flywheel lightened by a specialist called Pat Whittet down at Lightwater, and the car could live up to its official Bentley designation as 'the 100mph model'.

Progress in the Green Label was fascinating. The car was so much less ponderous than later models, so much better balanced, that steering it was almost a subconscious action. Thrilling to the engine note as it gathered speed, I relished the sense of developing urgency as it approached its maximum speed in second gear, which was just over 60mph. Continuing in third, the car seemed to gather itself rather like a hydroplane 'getting on to the step': the mudguards vibrated on their stays, the hard suspension (sternly checked by friction dampers) began to blend with the road surface, the crackle of the exhaust seemed to lose itself behind. It was like entering another world.

We were brought smartly back to this world by the difficulties Mother had in getting in and out. So sporting a car could only have appropriately styled mudguards, and there were no running boards, just a step attached to the chassis below the tiny door for the front passenger, and another beneath the equally tiny door on the opposite flank giving access to the rear seats. We had to carry a wooden stool for Mother to use as a mounting aid, but after she had barked her shins a couple of times (deliberately, I suspect) the car had to go. It had been a dream that lasted a fortnight.

It was also a useful lesson in what were desirable attributes. A good driving position (one could sit surprisingly far back from the wheel, with the gear lever alongside the right knee and the accelerator pedal between the clutch and the brake), close gearbox ratios, and a light flywheel which allowed the engine to respond quickly to the throttle – all these were things for which there was no substitute. The same was true of accurate high-geared steering, of stable snatch-free braking, of excellent all-round vision.

None of these virtues was likely to be found in the majority of cars then on the roads, cars which in substance or in spirit dated from the 1930s. Quite the nastiest of them to come into my hands – quite the most awful car that I ever drove – was a Flying Standard of about 1938. Some of its horrors were undoubtedly the products of inadequate maintenance, but its inherent flaws of design and construction deserved much of the blame for its appalling behaviour. Others of that generation of cheap tin boxes (more iron than tin, to be honest) were not much better.

Two exceptions were both Rovers. One was a low-powered pre-war open tourer, surprisingly refined in its demeanour and very quiet. I found it quite embarrassing to discover with its aid the difference between quietness and silence (that old business of comparative and absolute again), when I woke up to the fact that I was driving it more and more slowly, and even slower than that, in a subconscious attempt to get rid of that last tiny bit of noise. Never afterwards could I take seriously the Rolls-Royce claim for their 'Bentley' (the one built in Derby) as 'the silent sports car', nor for George Brough's claim for his pre-war car doing 'ninety in silence'. In cars on the move, silence is something that never happens.

The other Rover was an early post-war job belonging to my doctor, whose lovely daughter I taught to drive in it. Its bodywork, as a rather close-coupled mildly sporting saloon, was entirely individual and I thought it extremely handsome, intrinsically gentlemanly yet suggesting a panache not to be found in others where respectability took precedence over flair. Nor was it at all bad to drive, having a surprisingly positive gearbox (enhanced at will by a freewheel which could be selected to make clutchless gearshifts easy but eliminated engine braking) and quite decent brakes which were among the last examples of the American Bendix system to be used in British cars. Maybe the steering was not of the best, but this Rover had no bad habits and remained forbearing even when driven hard. I had huge fun with it one day in central London when all the buses were on strike and the traffic flowed unusually free and fast on the liberated streets: I tried out the theory, once promulgated by that redoubtable racing man Kenelm Lee Guinness (whose initials gave us KLG spark plugs), that the safest way to deal with crossroads was to go across as fast as possible since one would then be in the danger zone for the least possible time. It seemed to work . . . or maybe I was lucky.

The theory was one that I picked up from another renowned racing driver of earlier times, the late Dr Dudley Benjafield. When I was reading Laws at University College London, a fellow student and I (nearly all my friends were either from the Engineering faculty or from the Slade School of Fine Art, which must be indicative of something or other) set about reviving the pre-war United Hospitals and Universities of London Motor Club (otherwise known as Yoohoo) and went to see Dr Benjafield in his Harley Street lair. He very decently agreed to become Patron, came along and treated us to a talk about his days driving in the Bentley Team, and departed in his Citroën Light 15 by turning out of the quad into University Street, accelerating hard and shooting straight across Tottenham Court Road without a hint of hesitation. Maybe he, too, was just lucky.

He described the Citroën as 'the poor man's Bentley' – not that any of the Citroën boys, I suspect, was short of a bob or two – and even that helped us all in our veneration of good vintage cars and contempt for most of the shoddy things that came later. The Vintage Sports Car Club having defined 'vintage' as meaning pre-1931, I found it mildly amusing that most of the respectable cars I encountered were older than I was. My UCL friend, for example, had an Anzani-engined chain-drive Frazer Nash, while the chap who ran the workshop facilities for the engineering faculty, a charming fellow magnificently surnamed Baldhatchet, owned an utterly beautiful 1750 Alfa Romeo.

Bentleys abounded; after all, they could be bought in the early post-war years at about £100 per litre. A near neighbour who fancied himself an artist but who was actually a superb craftsman had a Blue Label 3-litre (the long-chassis touring affair with the frightfully wide-ratio B gearbox) on which he had built himself a splendid sporting open tourer body. He made it deliberately narrow because he and his wife were both tiny people; I could never have fitted into the driver's place, but I was skinny enough to be a passenger when he demonstrated quite remarkably powerful brakes. One night I was given the wheel of another friend's Bentley, one of the ten original short-chassis 4½-litre cars. I was on my own, while he enjoyed a drink at a local VSCC meeting, and was frankly irritated by the fact that whenever I urged the Bentley beyond 50mph the headlamps went out.

Of the other cars which regularly turned up at this local venue, the one I most admired was the low-chassis 2-litre OM cherished by a fast and naturally polished driver named Harry Cox. The side-valved six-cylinder engine was not very powerful, but the car was lightly built and superbly balanced. There was also a low-chassis 4½-litre Invicta in which I was taken for a brief but invigorating ride during which I discovered that peculiar sensation of drowning in air: with the wind-screen folded flat I had the full headwind in my face, and when I held my head at what proved to be an aerody-namically inadvisable angle the airflow stalled around my face and I found myself actually gasping for air, unable to breathe. Fortunately I was carrying my coke (or bowler, if you must) hat on my knees, and by shield-ing my face with that and breathing the still air within its crown I was able to recover my composure.

Another aerodynamic hazard presented itself when I was given a lift on the pillion of a Series C Vincent-HRD. Once a week its rider would dash from Bournemouth to Watford and back, and on this occasion was happy to take me from Sopley to Bagshot. This was in the days before crash helmets were common, and I was disconcerted to find that at 90mph my ears went into flapping resonance, tricked into vibration by the peculiarities of the turbulence behind the rider's head. Another memorable thing about that ride was that, despite the Vincent's footpegs being set quite high, I just sensed the outer edges of my shoe-soles feathering the road surface as we banked through a roundabout. Such performance! Such security! It was by appraising the ease of overtaking on the big Vincent that I understood the value of really good acceleration in the upper speed ranges. A murrain upon all this 0-60mph nonsense! What really matters is acceleration from 60 to 100 or more.

Despite all that, the next vehicle that I owned after the Morgan had so little performance that it could barely be measured. It would do 40mph and 40mpg, and although it could not be said to accelerate it could gradually gather speed. Since its brakes were feeble on dry roads and useless on wet ones it was not very good at losing speed either, and so provided very good training in the art of maintaining good average speeds by simply keeping going where others might slow or even stop.

This extraordinary little car was yet another product of the vintage era – a 1926 5CV Citroën, the 'Cloverleaf' model (*le trèfle*), with two slightly separated seats in front, a central one behind them, and a single nearside door which gave access to all three. I bought it for £25 from a chap who had been at school with me. When I went to look at it, he unlocked his garage door and there, beyond the car, was his fiancée working away at a hand loom. I suppose he locked her in and told her to get weaving . . .

It was a car of extraordinary simplicity: the axles were simply clamped to the extremities of long quarter-elliptic springs projecting from the chassis and devoid of any damping other than from the friction between their leaves. When negotiating a turn, initial roll would flatten the springs on the outside of the curve and allow those on the inside to curl, the result being to tighten the effective steering radius and thus initiate oversteer. Being undamped, the springs would promptly reflex , the consequence being understeer. It was like riding on one of those caterpillars which get along by alternately flexing and stretching their bodies, but in practice it meant that I just sat there and held the steering wheel still while the car did all its own steering corrections. It was quite hilarious – but the tyre grip was there, because this was the balloon-tyred version made when such fitments were just beginning to be fashionable. In fact the Cloverleaf proved able to complete three laps of a suburban roundabout in the time taken by a 1953 Hillman Minx to manage two.

As it happened I drove that Hillman quite a lot, and by its appropriate standards it was not a bad car, but there was a peculiarity in its braking system. In search of self-servo power the designers had given its brakes two leading shoes each: each shoe was pivoted at its rear, giving a self-wrapping tendency which enhanced the pressure of the shoe against the mating surface of the drum. It was a popular arrangement in those days for front brakes, but in the Hillman it was applied to the rear brakes as well. It followed that, when reversing, all the brakes responded with a negative servo effect, and the driver had to use a lot of leg muscle and a lot more anticipation.

In the Cloverleaf, artificially magnified braking effect was the speciality of the transmission brake, in a handsomely finned drum sandwiched between the back of the gearbox and the front of the torque-tube transmission. It followed that the braking torque was magnified by the final-drive gears in the back axle, but the effect was so vicious that it would lock the rear wheels if the road were at all damp. There were also drum brakes on the rear wheels (none at all at the front), and as originally conceived the hand lever and the pedal were separated in their communications with these two systems. However, a previous owner had coupled the two together so that the pedal operated all the brakes.

It made little difference. On wet roads the rear wheels

locked and the car went sliding merrily on, though directionally less stable than usual; on dry roads the total braking effect was terribly feeble. In vain might Tennyson cry 'Brake, brake, brake!': the exercise was pointless. There was one summery Sunday – it must have been Easter or Whitsun, for we were going to Goodwood (the nicest of all British motor racing venues) for the BARC meeting – when this matter came, as it were, to a head. My passengers were Ray Potter, later to become a motoring writer too, and a pretty young lady of his acquaintance. On our way south through Harringay (as it was then spelled) I saw the traffic lights turn treacherously red just before I reached them. 'I don't think we saw that, did we?' said I, judging that if I tried to stop I would end up stationary in the middle of the crossroads, and kept my foot on the accelerator pedal.

Just as we made it to the other side, a policeman sprang out of a doorway. He raised his arm and forefinger in an imperious gesture; he ran towards us, his eye firmly fixed upon his target; and, blinded by the urgency of duty, he ran full tilt into one of those tall steel columns which used to support the overhead wires for trolleybuses. I looked steadily straight ahead and Ray did likewise, but his girlfriend turned in her seat at the back and reported seeing him with his arms wrapped around the column and his knees folded in collapse. It would have been unkind to laugh, and indeed we were well into Sussex before I lost my fear of being crowded into the side of the road by a covey of police cars intent on revenge. Sorry, constable, I hope you suffered no lasting harm.

Ray Potter was another who, like my UCL chum, aroused my envy with an Anzani-engined Frazer Nash. Envy is something of which I cured myself at a fairly early age, and it did not last long in this case: I visited him once in the Cloverleaf and we swapped places. I felt real disappointment in the acceleration of his car, which was less lively than I had expected, while poor Ray felt blank consternation in discovering that my car had no acceleration at all.

It was never meant to have any. The little Citroën (like its eventual successor the 2CV, which rocked on its wheels in much the same way but did have brakes), when first presented in 1921, had been designed to endure the abuse of the meanest French peasant in a slow-moving agrarian setting, not for epic journeys. Its engine had a substantial light-alloy crankcase and a most impressively finned light-alloy sump (the French were the great pioneers of aluminium) but inside its robust iron cylinder block the pistons swept only $856cm^3$ past its side valves, and the true power amounted only to about 11bhp at a lowly 2100 rev/min. A very heavy flywheel kept it spinning, and the very wide ratios in the three-speed gearbox were a further deterrent to doing anything quickly, but the shifts were quite sweet when not using the clutch. For those times when I did use it, I devised a clutch-stop by bolting to the inside of the bell housing a piece of stout leather belting so positioned that, if the clutch pedal were fully depressed, the conical centre of the clutch driven plate would be pressed against it and thus braked. It worked: when I kicked the clutch pedal hard, I could make an upward gear change as fast as my hand could move the lever.

The Cloverleaf was not without its troubles, mainly in

the transmission brake and the cylinder-head gasket, and eventually I sold it to an acquaintance for £20. Within very few years it changed hands for more than £800, and after a few years more at over £2,000 – but that is not motoring, that is business.

It had been painfully clear to me that girls did not like the Cloverleaf. The fact that it offered them no protection from the weather was only one reason why, and reminds me that the maximum speed when protecting myself from heavy rain with an opened umbrella was impractically low at 18mph. It was also painfully clear to me that so long as I remained hard up I had no right to be consorting with girls anyway, and that a motorcycle seating only me would be a suitable deterrent to both sides. I had enjoyed riding my brother's vintage Triumph; I had enjoyed a friend's modern Ariel Red Hunter, a lively sporting 500 single with a sprung heel; but the motorcycle for which I had long and truly yearned was the Douglas Ninety Plus.

When it first appeared in 1949, it was the most modern motorcycle in the world – and this at a time when everywhere there were designers keen to whet their ambitions upon the stony face of tradition, to issue a futurist manifesto that would snatch the motorcycle out of its straits of habitual thinking and set it refreshed by novel forms and unfamiliar details upon a socially broadened and theoretically uninhibited new course. Unfortunately this movement, which had actually been evident by 1938 but had been stifled by the events of soon-succeeding years, was characterized more by stylistic effrontery than by engineering nicety; but the Douglas was outstanding in both respects, its appearance the natural and proper expression of the technical advances with which its specification bristled.

In vain might sniffy historians dismiss its fully-looped frame, trailing-arm rear suspension and horizontally-opposed twin-cylinder engine as mere echoes of the ABC which, designed by Granville Bradshaw a generation and a half earlier, had inspired BMW copyists to start making motorcycles. The Douglas was streets ahead of that as of everything else. Its springing was of progressive rate at both ends, by torsion bars for the rear and by taper-ground helical coils inside the tremendously rigid front forks with their leading bottom links. This was a chassis undaunted by obstacles: works riders used to demonstrate it by riding four times on and off a four-inch kerb at 30mph. Here was steering that needed no damper: customers might buy one for £3 extra, if only for the sake of appearances, but would soon learn never to let it interfere.

Here, moreover, was a machine which – by virtue of a low centre of mass, a comfortably long wheelbase and a structurally stiff chassis, all assuring excellent roadholding – could exploit really good brakes. Within the front wheel was a liberally finned and copiously ventilated drum brake of exceptional size: the total friction area of the brakes on the 90+ was, as I will ever remember, no less than 42 in^2, practically double what most bikes could offer, when even the big-twin Vincent – bigger, heavier and faster, and endowed with two brake-drums to each wheel – mustered only 36.

Exploiting such braking gave me many a chuckle. Having measured the bike's ability to stop at a rate of 1.2g (in 25ft from 30mph) and to do it repeatedly and reliably, I would come rushing up to T-junctions at such a speed that traffic on the main road would screech to a halt, convinced that this silly young man on his dangerous motorcycle could never stop in time and was about to have an accident. Thus offered a road clear of moving hazards, I could ride into the junction and away without hindrance. Alternatively, if the approaching driver was as silly as me and kept on coming, I could always stop in time.

That was when everything was in adjustment and working properly. When it was not, there was the most frightful judder which threatened to tear everything asunder, including the laws of probability. The Douglas was like that in most respects: life with it was a succession of brief episodes of utter bliss punctuating long and bewildering periods of fettling and frustration.

It was hardly to be wondered at. The design might have been good by the standards of its time (by which I mean particularly the use of stress-inducing lugs for joining the various tubes of the frame, for this was before the days of welded joints), but the thing was poorly made from shoddy materials – and that, too, was not surprising, for the 90+ was created at a time when the Douglas company was in receivership. The touring model, the Mark V upon which the 90+ was based, had been too modern in concept for the woefully ignorant and bitterly reactionary British motorcycling public of the day, and Douglas paid the price, ending a proud history (dating back to 1906) of good and much-loved motorcycles in the ignominy of making Vespa scooters under licence. Considering that the firm was in the hands of the receivers when the 90+ was born, it was a marvel that the poor thing should ever have seen the light of day.

Yet the makers contrived to give it an extensively reworked engine, happy up to 7500 rev/min and capable of at least 25bhp (which was a good 20 per cent more than the average road-going 350 in those days), with a flyweight clutch and a beautiful close-ratio gearbox behind it. The ability to reach 87mph in third gear, 77 in second and 55 in bottom gear far outweighed any question of what the Plus might be beyond the Ninety.

Ironically, the ride I most remember did not involve much of that sort of thing. One high summer day I was riding to Canterbury, where I had been engaged to

Setright c. 1951 in a Salmson San Sebastien Grand Prix
made in 1927. This car belonged to his brother.

play in a scratch orchestra (with some very good players in the wind sections) for a morning rehearsal and after-noon performance of Elgar's *The Dream of Gerontius* in the cathedral. With my clarinet strapped behind me I got almost to Rochester to encounter the tail of what proved to be a six-mile queue. As carefully as one does in such circumstances, I rode past it all – and was dismayed by the anger and hostility of all those stationary motorists, blaring their horns or even waving fists at me. There was no way in which I could have been harming them, but the thought that I was going and they were not aroused furious jealousy. Even on a good motorcycle, the world can be a sad place . . .

A lot of work was done on my Douglas, most of it necessary and all of it desirable, and I learned a few things in the process – most importantly, the need for good tyres. Of all the amendments I made, the most pro-ductive was to replace the original spidery steel wheels with 19-inch light-alloy racing rims and fit racing tyres, which I discovered made improvements to the steering and handling beyond all my expectations.

The tyres were the worst feature of my next motorcycle,

bought to keep me mobile at a time when I had quite despaired of the Douglas – though not so finally as to discard it. Bought new in 1960 (I never did repay Mother's loan, and still wonder whether she expected it), it was an Ariel Arrow, and once again it was derived from an exemplary modern design to which the British motorcyclist at large responded with his usual obstinate refusal to entertain nonconformist design. The Ariel Leader had a couple of years earlier been the most modern motorcycle ever – in the sense that the Citroën DS of 1955 was the most modern car ever. The most obvious of its attributes was the comprehensive weather protection (screen, fairing, and deeply valanced mudguards), intended to allow a rider to go out without being dressed like a deep-sea diver; but the most important was the pressed-steel chassis, formed as a monocoque backbone of generous proportions and admirable stiffness. Ariel did better business when they issued a 'naked' version, somewhat lighter and £30 cheaper, which they called the Arrow: the engine was the same simple $250cm^3$ two-stroke twin, and the bike still displayed the sprightliness and quick handling of the Leader.

It also displayed the miserable workmanship of the smug British industry which produced it: ovality of the brake drums and a general disposition to rust were the worst offences. Worse still was an error of judgement: when they specified 16-inch wheels and quite large-section tyres (at a time when skinny tyres on 19-inch wheels were the norm), they evidently feared that the typical British customer would blame them if the rate of tyre wear proved high. Accordingly, Dunlop were instructed to produce a tyre of hard-wearing specification, and the tread compound was therefore (since such was the trade-off in those days when the rubber industry still had plenty to learn) almost incapable of coming to grips with wet road surfaces. The Arrow would have me off and sliding down the road on my ear if someone so much as spat on the road. Racing people who adapted the Arrow for competition threw those nice little rims away and substituted nasty big conventional ones, because proper grippy tyres were available for them. I simply grew frightened of riding in the wet, and after a couple of years decided to get rid of the thing.

By that time I had taken a bigger and more momentous

decision. I had realized, after a couple of years at it, that the practice of the law did not suit me. As an academic subject I had found the law fascinating, but I hated its practical application, sullied with commerce, personal animosities, and onerous procedures serving no purpose but the perpetuation of some accident of history. Finding it so uncongenial, I realized at last that since I did not like it I should never be a success at it. At the end of 1960 I gave it up – one of the very best things I ever did – and prepared to make a fresh start.

2

NORMATIVE

On the first day of 1961 I became what I have remained ever since, a professional writer. A small publishing firm named Rowse Muir, specializing in technical journals, took me on as a staff writer for their monthly engineering magazine then called *Machine Age* – but already I feel the need for a motor-noter's digression, because the two partners who were my ultimate bosses were both motoring enthusiasts. Mr Rowse drove a Jaguar XK150, Mr Muir an Aston Martin DB2/4, and these two young gentlemen had in the 1950s produced – and may even have created – the monthly *Autocourse* magazine. I had not been a regular reader of it in the 1950s, it being a little too glossy for my pocket, but somehow a bound volume of 1953 found its way into my little office and I was struck by a photograph accompanying a road test of a Frazer Nash. It was a beautifully sharp picture of the nose of the car, liberally plastered with dead insects.

What eloquence! How better to portray a fast car than with this evidence of its speed on the open road! I wanted to see pictures of cars that had been driven fast through flood and tempest, over slush or sediment: the dried accretions of road dirt tell wondrous stories of aerodynamic virtues or deficiencies, tracing the lines of vortices and the wakes of detached and turbulent airflow. Such marvellously informative pictures could tell the shrewd beholder much that any verbal description could only approximate, just as a visual appraisal of the twin vortices at the tail of a car driven fast on wet roads can reveal much about overall aerodynamic drag. Does one see such things pictured?

One does not. All the pictures in the motoring press display cars in showroom condition, clean and shining with unsullied virtue, and the work of the motoring writer has been subordinated to the tyranny of the photographer, who will spend literally hours (having spent hours already finding a backdrop of appropriate architecture, suitable trees or rocky textures, or failing all that some mellifluously flowing contours of the open country) cleaning and polishing the car, angling it to suit the light that he calculates will fall at some specific future hour, removing licence discs and other post-showroom accretions, and generally showing what the customer will get when he buys it rather than when he drives it.

And why? Because the primary objective of the magazine is to gain revenue by gathering advertising. It was already evident in the 1960s that, because of the increasing resort of the public to television, people were more responsive to pictures than to text, any appreciation of which demanded some modest level of education and a longer span of concentration (or, at least, of attention) than the picture demanded. Regardless of the criticisms voiced by the hapless wretch who wrote the accompanying, and ever briefer, text, it was the pictures of the car which would seduce the 'reader' of the magazine and encourage him to be interested in the make and model under review. So, to please the manufacturer of the car – upon whose calculated bounty the magazine depended for the loan of the car for appraisal – the picture had to make the car look like a virgin prepared for her wedding rather than like a housewife trying to be all things to all her dependants. If it were done well, the manufacturer might be persuaded to buy advertising space and the magazine would prosper.

None of this affected me personally during my first few months in my new job. *Machine Age* reckoned to deal with all types of engineering except the agricultural and the pharmaceutical, but it was a controlled-circulation magazine which went into a lot of countries boasting a communist economy, so we excluded such capitalist indulgences as private cars and motorcycles. The effect of this on me was twofold: in the first place I was free to undertake appraisals of commercial vehicles, and in the second I could create no conflict of interests if I sought freelance work writing about private cars and motorcycles.

All went well. I learnt a great deal about publishing and about various kinds of engineering (to supplement what I had taken in through my pores as a son of an

Setright c. 1952/3 admiring an Alvis 12/50 with a four
cylinder Meadows engine. This belonged to a friend.

engineering family), and within fourteen months I was appointed editor of the magazine. I could then choose to interpret 'commercial vehicles' rather liberally. Thus I found myself trying a van version of the Reliant three-wheeler: the natural instability of its single-front-wheel layout led all too easily to lifting the inside rear wheel clear of the road when cornering energetically, as one did for example around Marble Arch. There was also a big BSA motorcycle equipped for police duties: the main snag was that everything in front of me mistook me for a policeman and drove very slowly, which even to a motorcycle can be surprisingly obstructive.

The freelance business grew encouragingly. One of the first road tests that I wrote was of an unusually interesting car, the Reliant Sabre. This fortunately had nothing whatever in common with the same firm's deplorable tricycle: it was a sharply styled open two-seater, originally designed by Reliant for manufacture in Israel, where it was known as the Sabra. The engine was that of the Ford 1.7-litre Consul, enough to give a lightweight car (the bodywork was all of fibreglass) quite lively performance, and the suspension was theoretically unsound but, since it allowed only a little movement of the wheels, quite harmless. What I liked most was the gearbox, a beautiful little four-speed affair with quite close ratios and light unbeatable synchromesh which allowed shifts to be made with lightning speed or without the clutch. This little jewel – even the lever controlling it felt like the work of a proudly committed craftsman – had been created to order by ZF in Germany. Whether the order emanated from Reliant or from Lotus is not certain, but I do not think that Reliant ever used enough examples to exhaust the production run, and the same was certainly true of those few examples which found their way into the best examples of the Lotus Type 14 Elite.

Was there ever a car more beautiful than that Elite? I collected a test example from the Lotus factory, then at Cheshunt, and was soon asking myself whether there were ever a car more heart-rending in its inability to behave as beautifully as it looked. The fallibility of early examples was already notorious, but after the construction of the fibreglass bodies was taken over and refined by Bristol (who did it with their usual exquisite care) there were still mechanical flaws galore in the machinery. My test specimen vibrated badly and overheated outrageously, but it did demonstrate all the advantages of light weight, and it did show that exemplary roadholding was not incompatible with a luxurious ride. I was surprised by the steering being so low-geared, and overall I felt disappointed. For many others, I suspect the biggest disappointment was the fact that a high-specification Elite cost slightly more than that new popular paragon, the E-type Jaguar.

It was in the summer of 1963 that a spotless 3.8 E-type coupé was delivered to my Hampton front door at exactly 0830h. I had been living there two years, and this very gentlemanly delivery driver was the first person ever to keep an appointment with me there punctually. What time he set out I do not know, but even earlier in the day the Jaguar PRO, Bob Berry (a competent racing driver in D-types), would have taken the car out on the road to verify its speed capability and check that everything was in order.

Later in this book I shall give an account of what, in this car, was to prove one of the most memorable drives of my career, but I cannot forbear to state now that I found the Series 1 E-type a most impressive piece of machinery as well as uncommonly good-looking. Jaguar always spent their money where it would show, and in the E-type this would include the under-bonnet view, where the camshaft covers and carburettor tops were polished and the exhaust manifolds stove-enamelled in a lustrous deep blue. Even the dipstick was ostentatiously knurled where one was supposed to grasp it, though to attempt it when the engine was hot would burn your fingers. Much of that oppressive under-bonnet heat (there was an enormous lot of iron in the Jaguar block) came through into the cabin where, in the Series 1, there was a serious shortage of room for a tall driver. If some of that heat could have reached the brakes it would perhaps have done them some good: they did not work effectively when cold because Sir William Lyons flatly refused to spend an extra three-farthings per wheel on superior pads which would have solved the problem. He also drove a hard bargain on dampers, at fifteen shillings each.

All Jaguars, so long as the business was in the grim Lyons grip, were like that. Costly-looking leather was cheaply held in place by stationer's staples where they would not show. Electrics were made by Lucas with the same cynicism as Lyons employed in ordering them. Yet the E-type could not help but seem special: all other Jaguars that I tried, at that time and for long afterwards, were clearly pretentious heaps of cheaply made junk masquerading as high-performance luxury cars, and they were commercially very successful because they attracted the sort of customers at whom they were aimed; but the original E-type did motoring a great service, not merely by creating a furore (though it certainly did that when it appeared) but by effecting a new emancipation.

It was popularly seen as supremely symbolic just at the time when people were beginning to recognize that their cars could serve as status symbols. It was popularly described as looking phallic, just at that moment in the early 1960s when people were thirsting for the opportunity to employ such imagery in their conversations.

What it most crucially did, at a price that was typical of Jaguar and therefore far below what was demanded by the likes of Aston Martin or Ferrari, was to enable a man (or, better still, a woman) to discover that to drive at 140mph did not require the abilities of a superman (or, Heaven forbid, a superwoman) nor the wealth of a Croesus. By its sheer availability and its simple drivability the E-type achieved a salutary debunking of the mythology of speed. Indeed, it destroyed the very images it created.

How much more the imagery mattered than the reality was demonstrated by the continued success of the E-type in its later forms. When the engine was painfully enlarged to 4.2 litres it could no longer be run safely to such high rates of revolution, so the car was actually slower. Acquiring some early radial-ply tyres perhaps improved its low-speed ride a little, but the handling was never again as finely balanced as it had been on the original highly developed bias-ply tyres. The only clear improvements were to interior comfort, and the substitution of a new and fairly decent gearbox in place of the heavy and atrociously inept gearbox (made in the Midlands by Moss Gears and already of some antiquity) that drivers of the early 3.8 had to suffer.

As the years went on, the E-type became more a very fast tourer, less a sports car – and I must confess that, unfashionable though it was to admit it when the thing evolved in 1966, I expressed a liking for the long-wheel-base 2+2 with a mere 3-speed automatic transmission by Borg-Warner. If it were more suitable than the original car for touring I was not going to object, and since I found that I could hold it in a mild and stable drift through Woodcote corner on the old Silverstone GP circuit at 105mph, it was by touring-car standards eminently fast.

Just a decade after the debut of the 3.8 E-type, it metamorphosed into the Series 3 version propelled by an elegant V12 engine of 5.3 litres that was little heavier than the original in-line six. It was now emphatically not a sports car, and I liked it the more for that: the degree of civilization implicit in the idea of a touring car had much more appeal when combined with unquestionably high performance, and this car had that. During the original launch of this model my co-driver somehow contrived to spin it without trying, but I found it perfectly manageable and amenable to brisk driving. Alas, it was still manifestly a Jaguar, and therefore never above suspicion.

Back in the early 1960s, when I was beginning to establish myself, there were plenty of lesser cars which were honest in their mediocrity but nevertheless revealed standards of behaviour notably higher than had their counterparts in the previous decade. The obvious paragon was the Mini, which was in a class by itself: it was never comparable with anything else, and should never have been seen as competing with anything else. By the time that it acquired decent brakes, as it did in the Cooper S version, it was a very convincing little brick indeed, too harsh for long journeys but enormous fun otherwise. Entirely different in character was another small front-driver, the Renault 4, which emerged in 1961 as a perfect example of logical French parsimony: if all its windows were of flat glass, the view through them would suffer no distortions. It swayed like a sailing dinghy in corners, but it had the world's first sealed cooling system, and it took many long years and many even longer miles (it was certainly not a fast car) before, as in many cases, it broke apart in the middle.

A small car which felt as though it were breaking apart in the middle, although it had in fact a cruciform chassis of decent strength, was the Triumph Herald. It was the independent rear suspension by swinging half-axles which created this unwelcome impression, which could be succeeded in inept hands by an accident of daunting complexity. In other respects it was an admirable design, with all its body panels detachable for ease of repair, and styling (by the industrious and versatile Michelotti) of considerable chic – and when, as in the case of the Vitesse, it was endowed with a little in-line six-cylinder engine, there were performance and refinement into the bargain. As for the handling, I found (as with many cars) that hyperinflation of the tyres cured a lot of ills: in the case of the 12/50 Herald, for instance, I set all the tyres at 35 lb/in^2 with satisfying results. This was at a time when most manufacturers recommended 24 lb/in^2, and

Triumph specified very different pressures at front and rear. However, I had noted at various test days on racing circuits such as Goodwood and Silverstone that most manufacturers then inflated their cars' tyres to somewhere in the region of 38-40 lb/in^2, and that was a pointer worth following.

This trick did not have much effect on the behaviour of the VW Beetle, which likewise had swinging half-axle rear suspension, which was (to be fair to Professor Rumpler, whom I believe to have first devised it) originally a German idea. I believe that the rubber of its tyres, as in the case of my Ariel Arrow, had been compounded with hard wear as a priority, and like the Arrow it had little grip on wet roads. In other respects – notably the flat-four engine (as near to perfect balance as could be economically achieved), the free use of lightweight magnesium alloys, the ability to wheel the whole engine and final drive out of the tail when there was work to be done, the slick early non-synchro gearbox, and above all the rigorous bare-knuckle elimination of everything unnecessary – the early post-war VW deserved a generous measure of admiration.

It was all very well admiring these things, but the admiration had always to be qualified by the recognition that they were not actually good cars, merely cars that were better than one might have expected. It did not follow that they were good enough for Setright, by now feeling sufficiently established (and in financial matters sufficiently confident, for I was now earning as much as my father did a quarter of a century earlier, even if the intervening inflation made nonsense of the comparison) to consider what car to procure for personal use.

Because of the high regard that I had for myself (and it did not matter to me that others – what could they know? – might not share it) it would have to be good. It would have to steer impeccably, go and stop reasonably fast, have roadholding and handling of a high order, be comfortable and if possible elegant. It should be able to seat four, even if it might not often have to do so. It should not be inordinately costly to fuel and maintain. Finally, if it were not to invite continual reproach, it would have to be of good quality.

This last matter narrowed the choice considerably.

It would mean, amongst other things, that I should have to buy a used car rather than a new one but, since it is implicit in good quality that the thing should remain good despite having been used, that ought not to be a serious objection. The serious difficulty lay in establishing what cars were, or had in the recent past been, truly good: the list looked pathetically short. Nothing could be considered from the USA, nothing from Italy, and certainly nothing from Germany, despite the professionally cultivated aura of respectability surrounding the products of Daimler-Benz. Sadly nothing from France, where native and politically fomented antipathy to anything savouring of aristocracy had sent all the makers of the princely cars we had once so admired to the ever-ready economic guillotine. The cars of Japan were not yet ready to be considered, even though some of Honda's motorcycles showed the direction they might take. What, apart from Britain, did that leave?

Spain? In the factory that had once been the source of Hispano-Suiza cars of blessed memory and was now building ENASA buses, the best apprentices were set to producing parts – no matter how long it took them, nor how many were rejected before one passed muster – for the Pegaso. Designed by the lordly and academic Wilfredo Ricart (the first man ever to draw up the ideal geometry for a De Dion rear axle, and the only one ever to see it produced), the Pegaso had an exquisite specification and was beautifully made, even if some of the bodies created for it by fashionable European coachbuilders did it a disservice. Alas, in the seven years of Pegaso production from 1951, only about 125 cars were built: I doubt if any was a four-seater, and servicing and maintenance in Britain in the 1960s would have been somewhere on the scale between nightmarish and impossible.

For all these reasons, rather than for any patriotic cause, my car would have to be British. In the hungry sellers' market that Britain had become after all those years of wartime and post-war austerity, most British cars were poorly made and many of them, from the lesser Austins to the swanky Daimlers and Armstrong-Siddeleys, were pretentious rubbish. Alvis did rather better, but their engines and steering were poor. Aston

Martin tried hard to do better still, but their development was not as good as their design and their reputation for being troublesome was pervasive. That left Bristol and Rolls-Royce.

Seen in that blessedly simple reduction, the choice was surprisingly easy to make. There could be no question of my having a Rolls-Royce. Quite apart from not wanting to be seen as one of those people (the majority of the firm's customers, I fear) who simply, automatically and uncritically bought a Rolls-Royce because they liked to be seen as the sort of people who did just that, I had considerable experience of the cars that the company had produced, and it gave me ample grounds to excuse myself from the dubious distinction of being an owner.

By this time my brother had become a man of some note in the rubber industry, and it had suited his purposes to employ, partly as a mobile boardroom, a Mark 6 Bentley. As a product of the R-R car factory set up in Crewe after the war, it was a curiously contradictory apparatus: the interior appointments were impressive and the action of the gearbox with its suavely sliding lever close to the driver's right knee was truly refined – but the engine was a dismally retrogressive F-head affair derived from a heavily compromised military series, the steering was mushy, and in place of the elegant centre-lock wheels which could once have been taken for granted there were crude disc wheels garnished with gay-deceiver nave-plates, at whatever cost to brake cooling.

Ah, those brakes. For years to come, R-R would continue to reply to critics demanding something more modern such as disk brakes, then considered remarkable for their freedom from fade, that 'Rolls-Royce drum brakes do not fade.' They were right: their brakes were set up with trailing shoes garnished with heat-resistant linings as brittle as china, their low coefficient of friction compensated by strong support from the servo. The Rolls-Royce servo, however, was itself driven from the gearbox by a friction clutch – and that, as I found in a hurried journey from Southampton to London, could and did fade.

I do not suppose that it was the prospect of entering at high speed a slow roundabout in an apparently brakeless two-ton car that put my father off when he cavilled at the R-R servo. It was more probably the fact that, at very low speeds as when parking, the drive from the gearbox introduced a delay in brake application which could be measured as about 18 inches. If an R-R is a very solid device it is also a very costly one, and not really suitable for hitting anything even at walking speed. And what if (perish the thought) the car were to hit *another* R-R?

The Mark 6 Bentley made way for the best R-R that I have ever encountered. It has long saddened me that I never drove one of the Derby-built Bentleys (in the old days we all called the 1930s 3½-and 4¼-litre machines Rolls-Bentleys, an expression to which R-R took exception in their characteristically sniffy way), for I reckon that they must have been the very nicest cars to bear the name; but there was a softer-tuned version with radiator to match known as the 25/30hp R-R, and it was one of these (there were never many, for the model only stayed in production for two years) that my brother found. It was handsomely bodied by Park Ward, was exquisite in construction and manners, sensibly dimensioned and adequately fast. All the earlier 'small' Rolls-Royce cars had been embarrassingly slow – when I tried an early Light Twenty I thought it almost as sluggardly as my Cloverleaf Citroën – and distressingly inferior in handling and roadholding, but this one had, as R-R would say, 'enough' power.

As Setright has often said, 'enough' is only just enough; more than enough is enough. If the 25/30 had enough power (not being as sadly overbodied as many, this one could work its way up to 80mph), it was certainly not over-endowed: this was not a car in which to try joining mainstream traffic on an arterial road from standstill in a side-street. That was something my brother had to do on a daily basis, and he substituted an S1 Bentley, which could do just that even if its other merits were less easy to identify.

All the many Rolls-Royce cars that I sampled at that time and in later years, from a P1 Continental up to one of the last from Crewe, have disappointed me in some way or other. One can respect them for what the firm sought to maintain, and for some of what they achieved; one might even approve of their increasing tendency to produce cars made in imitation of American mechanical design and using more and more American components, for by the time of the S1 (or Silver Shadow, if you chose the R-R clone of the Bentley) the USA owned half of the world's cars. But American cars need to be made by American machinery, putting American iron through American foundries and using American factory methods, in which case they can be the quietest and most hospitable cars in the world. Try to adapt such designs to Derbyshire men and Cheshire methods, and the result may well recall some of the Biblically forbidden aspects of mule-breeding.

So it seemed that my choice was that of Hobson: I should have to have a Bristol. Considering that I had no personal experience of Bristol cars this might seem rash, but I had read extensively and observed carefully. In the 1950s I had seen the Bristol team of 2-litre cars regularly winning their class (while looking better-behaved than anything else on the track) in the one-hour production-car races staged annually at

The favourite 1955 Bristol 405.

Silverstone. I had stood and watched with admiration growing to awe as, in the objective quiet of 3 a.m., somebody flung a Bristol 403 in a long, stable, and magnificently uncompromising, high-speed drift through the Neasden bends of London's North Circular Road. Evidently it deserved its reputation as a driver's car.

My researches into aircraft and aero-engine manufacture had confirmed that the Bristol Aeroplane Company, who produced it, were probably unique in their qualification (having both the competence and the temperamental inclination) to make the best car in the world. Whatever might be said against R-R and others for adopting alien ideals and methods, I had no doubt that although the mechanical design of the Bristol was known to be based on work done before the war by BMW, Bristol would have subjected it to such rigorous revision in everything from metallurgy to morphology as would elevate the Bristol to a far superior plane.

That is indeed what Bristol did. However, this cannot be the place for me to recite the intricacies of design and development which inspired my desire and lasting love for their cars. I have surely written enough about them already: one of my books on them ran to 120,000 words. Time may prove that not to have been enough, but at the time it seemed more than enough.

When I began to consider what Bristol I might get, the word 'enough' loomed most ominously over the amount that I could afford. As I had recognized, to buy a new one was impossible to contemplate – and in any case by 1961, after savage treatment by government trimming the aviation industry to its needs, Bristol had found it necessary to abandon the manufacture of its own engines and gearboxes and to adopt some from Chrysler, which made the new Bristol 407 rather an unknown quantity. However, depreciation being what it then was when only owners realized how good Bristols were, it was possible to buy a Bristol 401 with a decade (and possibly 100,000 miles) behind it for about the price of a new Mini; that, it seemed, was where I should start.

So I addressed myself to Mr Anthony Crook in these

terms, and one of his gentlemanly salesmen showed me what was available, allowing me a brief drive just to get the feel of it – in the course of which I instructively hung the tail out a little on the roundabout in front of his showrooms. He then undertook to give my needs some thought, and a few days later reversed into the front drive of my house in a wondrously clean black 401. In some respects it had been updated (a procedure that Bristol always encouraged), so it had the front suspension with anti-roll bar, and the big Alfin front brakes, of the later 403 model. It was unusual in the cabin too, quite apart from having radio speakers front and rear: like very few other 401 or 403 specimens it avoided the conventional fancy woods for the dashboard, using instead panels machined from slabs of Tufnol.

Now who remembers Tufnol? Like a number of other wonder materials of the post-war period, such as Paxolin which also figured in the Bristol's substructure, it was an engineering material much used by the aviation industry (though by no means exclusively) and owing much to developments in the plastics industry. Tufnol was a wooden laminate that was impregnated with a thermosetting resin (akin to Bakelite) at very high pressure, giving it remarkable mechanical properties. Harder and tougher than any 'natural' wood, it was also kinder to the touch and to the eye, with a surface for which any proponent of eggshell lacquers would have given his eye teeth.

I really must try not to drift off into raptures over all the detail felicities of the Bristol, though there be scope for miniature essays on dozens of items between (and including) the bumpers: the locking system, the rear window, the suspension geometry, the dampers, the switches, the throttle linkages . . . Even the list would be too long, let alone worthy treatment of all that appeared in it. Just let me enter this caveat now, to be read as applicable to all Bristols: many of them differ in detail from others apparently similar, and very rare indeed are the critics (especially among the motoring journalist fraternity) whose judgement based on one specimen can be trusted.

There was for example the young lad who ventured a 'test' of a 2-litre car for one of the popular classic-car monthlies, who bemoaned his difficulties in heel-and-toe driving because of an ill-placed accelerator pedal. He did not know that the pedal is adjustably mounted on a cross-shaft carried in ball bearings, so that its position can be varied in elevation and azimuth to suit any driver, though it would have been initially set to suit the original owner. Much the same applies to criticisms that I have read of damper settings, in models ranging from the 411 to the current Fighter: these can be adapted to meet the preferences of the customer, as can the driving position and much else. A manufacturer who applies a self-imposed production limit of three cars a week – or, in the case of the Fighter, twenty a year – can do these things, and does them when asked. Someone attuned to the cloned immutability of a Ford or a Peugeot or some such may fail to understand, let alone appreciate, such indulgence of individual whims, and indeed why should he know better?

So there I was with this lovely 401-as-amended and, as I quartered the country in it, a growing appreciation of just how good a really good car could be. The surprise (which grew with the experience) was in the fact that it took time to learn how to use the car. I do not think that I flatter myself in believing that I can get the hang of any modern car (anything later than 1940 indeed) in a day or so, and more often than not in an hour or so; but a Bristol needs a week.

At first sight it is a very straightforward car. It is only that most admirable of human impulsions, curiosity, which reveals how very subtle the Bristol is. We may therefore forgive those who, coming new to one, find it daunting. They have heard that it is a 'driver's car', but that does not mean that it is twitchy and dramatic. It is nothing of the sort: it is smooth and self-effacing at any level of performance a driver might choose within a considerable envelope. Nor is there any implication that the driver must be highly skilled or intelligent to obtain good results. The car does much to make his task easy and his operation efficient: all the controls are acceptably weighted, and everything is in the right place – especially the driver himself. You do not have to work hard at driving it, but you do have to work long.

It is not a car that you can fully exploit at your first meeting; you will need time to learn what it can do. Time is of the essence: it is almost entirely a matter of timing, of growing familiar with the unique Bristol rhythm. It is dictated by spring rates and tyre sidewalls, by the distribution of masses and the precession of poles; it is as dependable as the motions of a mechanical clock, as naturally assimilated as the motion of a garden swing – but the necessary familiarity with it takes time to acquire. Once you have done it, you can drive a Bristol well; as you continue, you learn that there are ways whereby the driver can begin to dictate to the car, not just depend on its natural behaviour. You find that you always know exactly what it is going to do next, in response to whatever you demand; and so in due course the driver becomes authoritarian, goes through a brief phase of being a bully, and eventually emerges as boss. He can now drive a Bristol very well indeed.

I reckon that I managed pretty well in some others, too. The repertoire of Mini-tweaks, including the flick turns through 90, 180 and 360 degrees, came readily, for instance. In fact that sort of thing was surprisingly easy in quite a lot of cars of that period, probably because they were inadequately shod. The only time I recall going adrift was in a front-drive Alfasud, because I had omitted noting that the handbrake worked on the front wheels! No harm was done (it was in an extensive greensward), except to my *amour propre* in the presence of a carload of giggling school-girls . . . As to the Mini, I have to admit that I admired it much more than I liked it, which makes an interesting counterpoint to the fact that I liked its designer, the late Sir Alec Issigonis, much more than I admired him.

Counterpoint is not the same as contrast. Few vehicles could be more removed from the Mini than the big road-haulage lorries plying our roads, but in the early 1960s they too were undergoing changes that were as revolutionary as anything that Issigonis achieved. The traditional British lorry had a rigid frame with four, six or eight wheels and an engine chosen with low running costs as the absolute priority. The British transport industry (which presented a pretty formidable lobby whenever legislation loomed) was obsessed with profit and utterly indifferent to all else, including safety. Burst tyres resulting from gross overloading were an everyday occurrence, and the slowness of heavily laden goods vehicles on the roads was infuriating for everybody else. I remember road-testing a Dennis six-wheeler, the pitifully feeble engine of which was incapable of hauling the vehicle's maximum rated load up the main-road incline past The Devil's Punchbowl on the arterial A3 road to Portsmouth in any gear higher than second. I felt acutely embarrassed, bitterly frustrated, and eventually thoroughly angry, as the hapless queue of cars behind grew longer and longer. There might conceivably be some case for imposing maximum speed limits on road vehicles on certain roads, but for load vehicles I argued that there should be minimum speeds, to ensure the fluidity of traffic. It was sheer arrogance for the road haulage industry to pretend that only their business was road business.

There was one firm that was an exception to the general rule: Foden, who built some very high-grade eight-wheelers, had a good and clever engineer named

Jago who schemed really powerful engines. One that I remember fondly was a 4½-litre in-line six with two-stage forced induction, the first stage being by engine-driven Roots supercharger and the second by exhaust-driven turbocharger, and it gave more power and torque for less weight than conventional jobs of 9 or 11 litres.

However, the traditional British lorry was soon to be a thing of the past. The increasing popularity in mainland Europe of the articulated truck, where a tractor tugged a semi-trailer which could be replaced at any convenient depot by another – and especially when this arrangement was combined with the use of the newly standardized containers – led to a strong demand for such vehicles (far bigger and more powerful than ours) to be admitted to Britain, and for similar British vehicles to share the roads of island and mainland alike. It called for a lot of new legislation, but it was inevitable that it should happen.

One of the results was that our motorways, not intended to serve mainly as goods channels, became clogged with trucks, admittedly faster than our old lorries used to be but still obstructive. Another was that when one of these articulated affairs had an accident, it was usually a complex and hideous mishap in which the whole vehicle would fold like a jackknife around the hinge in its middle. Another was that the railways and canals lost a lot of goods business, and we may yet reflect upon the fact that the most prosperous European countries are those in which a significantly smaller proportion of goods haulage is done by road.

Possibly less significant among the consequences of this change was that Setright should now find himself testing artics. I did not greatly mind, nor was I greatly moved. The one thing that really impressed me in these heavy vehicles was the petite and precise lever, like a cherry on a stick, which served as a finger-light parking brake, for it merely controlled a valve which allowed the escape of the compressed air which held back the spring which would otherwise apply the brakes. Ruefully I compared it with the clumsy great lever, invariably ill-placed and involving all the wrong muscles, which the driver of an ordinary private car is expected to use not only for parking but also as an emergency brake of last resort should the foot-brakes fail. This dreadful contraption seems to be an inheritance from railway practice, or even from horse-drawn carriages, and car designers seem oblivious to the notion that the lever should at least be pushed rather than pulled. I have on one occasion been able to persuade a manufacturer to locate it more effectively, but that little cherry-on-a-stick would be much nicer.

There was little pleasure otherwise to be found in driving commercial vehicles, although the automatic preselector transmission of a double-decker bus was impressive. Not so its brakes: in those days it was actually perfectly legal for a motorist to go uninsured provided that he deposited £10,000 with the Bank of England as surety for any claims (I knew somebody who did it, just for the fun of telling interfering policemen that he had no insurance!) and London Transport exploited this for their own ends, in effect becoming their own insurers. They then deduced that it would cost them less to run over some little old lady in the street than to suffer a busload of claims from passengers with broken arms or heads suffered when braking hard to avoid the said old lady; they therefore required that all their buses, though capable of meeting legal requirements (which were not strenuous) in braking ability, should not be capable of significantly more abrupt braking. The heavy vehicle operators' concern for profit was in those days (and maybe still is) quite astonishing.

They were a tricky bunch. I recall measuring a very respectable level of lateral acceleration (think of it as cornering power) in some 15-tonner that I once tested; the test load was of very high-density material (slabs of cast iron, if I remember correctly) so that it lay low on the load platform, keeping the centre of gravity of the whole as low as possible – a situation quite unlike the normal carriage of more bulky goods, which would raise the centre of gravity considerably and increase the likelihood of the whole lot falling over if one tried to take a corner fast. Then there were display days when Leyland would offer all their current HGVs for trial around their rather splendid figure-of-eight test track up in Lancashire.

They were not laden heavily, and I felt quite uninhibited in flinging an artic through the underbridge bend in what onlookers insisted was a drift. We all knew about the four-wheel drift as practised by the drivers of racing cars in those days, but a ten-wheel drift did seem a trifle extreme.

The last straw in my dealings with the HGV trade was when Ford invited me to try an experimental tractor powered by a gas turbine. This I thought an excellent idea, and it was with more than the usual enthusiasm that I set out on the roads of Essex in an artic pulled by this gas turbine, which I found very well-behaved, blessedly powerful, and more controllable than I had expected. On some roads I did feel inhibited, however, by a certain choppiness in the suspension of the tractor, whose dampers were probably set up for American rather than British roads, and I said so in the piece that I wrote afterwards. It was explanation rather than criticism, for the thing was after all only a prototype and by no means something ready to be put on the market – yet my shocked editor insisted on expunging my comment, declaring that the magazine must not impair its good relationship with Ford's advertising department by publishing any such criticism of the ride quality. I was disgusted, and never wrote for that commercial vehicle magazine (or indeed any other) ever again.

'So why,' the astute reader asks, 'was Setright writing for a specifically commercial-vehicle magazine when such vehicles came under his ambit in his own magazine?' The fact is that by this time I had left *Machine Age* behind me. Mr Rowse and Mr Muir, I had begun to notice, were barely speaking to each other; they no longer shared even a lunch, let alone jointly presiding over our monthly editorial meetings. I forecast that the business was doomed, and chose to leave rather than to await being left. My forecast was correct: six months after my departure, the firm folded.

It was my fascination with tyres that put my feet under a new desk. So enthusiastic had my study of them been that I probably knew more about them than anyone else outside the industry; this may not have been saying a lot, since at that time nobody outside the industry appeared to care a hoot about the things, but it sufficed to get me a job with a public relations agency in London who had just secured the account of the Firestone Tyre & Rubber Company.

It could not have been a more exciting time to be involved. What deserves to be recalled as 'the radial-ply revolution' led by Michelin and Pirelli was beginning to take effect in Europe, where several major car manufacturers were beginning to recognize the advantages inherent in this new type of tyres and to adapt their new car designs to suit them. On the other hand, and especially in the USA, there were many men with factories full of obsolete machinery for making the familiar old bias-ply tyres, and doubtless with bellies full of ulcers as a result, who were anxious to resist the impending and predictably costly change by all possible means.

Firestone, though as American as any, were ready to go with the flow, starting with their smaller European plants and leaving the huge American ones for a while because they knew that the American car-makers would postpone all engineering changes as long as they could.

They had some particularly clever technicians at the time, which helped them on two fronts: they were introducing one of the best current radials for ordinary cars (in European sizes) and they were entering top-class motor racing with new tyres of unconventional construction and revolutionary dimensions, starting the trend to wide low-profile tyres that has developed steadily ever since.

This led to my writing a lot of educational stuff about tyres, and to my travelling all over the show in Europe to follow what was going on at the major racing venues, not only Grand Prix F1 racing but also the most important sports car events. In the process, I took in a great deal that had nothing to do with cars.

For instance, the opening F1 race of the 1966 took place one fine Sicilian Sunday in the spring, preceded by a 1,000km race for sports cars at Monza in northern Italy on the previous Monday. I flew out to Milano for the Monza affair but afterwards, having plenty of time in hand, chose to travel to Syracusa by train. It would mean covering the length of Italy in three stages, but I should see a lot that otherwise I might forever miss.

The first leg was the most emotional. On Tuesday morning I sauntered into the big railway terminus in Milano, a building full of monumental and rather pompous modernity, created to celebrate Mussolini's Fascist makeover of the nation. I never aligned myself with the popular despisal of Mussolini and his brand of authority, for it seemed quite wrong that he should be tarred with the same brush that Hitler undoubtedly deserved. Apart from making the trains run on time, Mussolini did a lot for Italy after coming to power in 1922, and one only had to pay attention to what he said to realize that he did not share Hitler's mindset. When the Nazis took control of Germany in 1933, Mussolini declared: 'We should be pleased, I suppose, that Mr Hitler has carried out a revolution along our lines; but they are Germans, and they will be ruining our idea.'

As I strolled into the station, I heard the strains of a fine military band. Some visiting general was just departing by train, and there on the platform was the band of the Bersaglieri in full feather, and the railway-station acoustics could not mask the most crisp and brilliant brass articulation I had ever heard. Finding my way to my correct platform I could not expect more music, but neither did I expect such quietness as enveloped me as I boarded my train. This was the famous *Settebello*, the crack express of the day, and after the clunky ancient rolling stock of post-war British Railways it was a revelation. The interior was furnished in horizon blue and trimmed in glass and aluminium, and as the doors closed themselves with the shockless finality of dying eyelids all external noise was barred from my compartment. Only my eyes could tell me when we began to move, how urgently we accelerated out of the station, and with what prodigious speed we flew like a hushed rocket along (but so smoothly that we could not really have been touching?) the track to Firenze.

I had an evening and a morning to take in that astonishing city. I walked the mediaeval streets and squares, stood in the Loggia dei Lanzi to gawp at Perseus and David, went into the Uffizi to take in its contents, marvelled that the chance should have been given me to see what I had read about in school become reality. The walls of my school had been covered in reproductions of classical paintings, and throughout my year in the fifth form I sat beneath that famous painting of Dante catching his first sight of Beatrice. Now, tracing the banks of the Arno, I stood where he had stood, saw the Ponte Vecchio looking much as he had seen it (though the retreating Germans did some damage). I lifted my eyes to the hills and saw Browning's lovely Fiesole. I was enchanted.

No such experience was possible in Roma, where I alighted from my second train. The place was too big, I had too little time: a brisk walk to view a brace of fountains and then I was off on the last leg of my journey – and what a different train, what a different experience! Here were clankings, flies, and plain wooden seats – but somebody must have known about seat design, for I was never uncomfortable throughout the long, long day as the train trundled slowly down the coast. Leaving the capital it had run for miles alongside the ancient Roman aqueduct; further south it ran sometimes so close to the sea that I could look down on children playing in some little rocky cove. At Napoli it took a wide detour inland

and stopped for a while outside the city, while I recalled my classics master saying that although according to popular usage one may 'see Naples and die', one had but to smell Naples and you would die! Why we stopped where we did I do not know, but I had never seen such extensive slums, such a saddening shanty town. Some of my neighbours in Highbury in the 1930s had been refugees from this area around 1920; now I could see why.

This is one of the great things that powered transport has done for us, enabling us to go and enquire into the world beyond our immediate ken, to observe the things in it that matter, the beautiful things and the terrible things. It was a motor car (a BMW 7-series, not that it matters) that enabled me to see similar degredation, possibly on a larger scale, near Madrid airport: the difference was that this was thirty years later, which made it somehow less excusable.

Night had fallen on my torpid Italian trundler by the time we reached the toe of Italy, and the passenger coaches were shunted on to the ship which ferried us across the straits of Messina. I stood out on deck, leaning over the railings, wondering at the depth of the waters' inky blue-blackness, astonished by the contrasting fluorescent white of the foam on the bow wave, seduced by the warmth and brilliance of the night sky on the latitude of the Holy City. I was utterly enchanted. I took no notice of anything else that night as we made our way down the Sicilian coast to Syracusa, but next day I was basking in the same sun as vitalized the little basilisk-eyed lizards on the rocky walls around the ancient Greek amphitheatre just outside the town, close to the roads on which the Gran Premio di Siracusa would soon engage my attention.

It was the most southerly of the races I attended that year, the most northerly (and appropriately different) being at Karlskoga in Sweden. The business part of this was a F2 event, but one of the supporting races was for an extraordinarily mixed bunch of cars of which the impressively original Bugatti T35 of Hamish Moffat, proceeding in rousing but evidently controllable four-wheel drifts on its very slender beaded-edge tyres, was locked in stern battle with a F2

Connaught. Talking with Mr Moffat (already known as a highly adventurous young gentleman in the Lagonda Club) in the paddock, I hazarded some enquiry about what the Bugatti was like to drive and, to my amazement, he promptly invited me to climb in and try it!

This was easier said than done: I had to remove my shoes, but found that the slender pedals fitted beneath my stockinged feet well enough. A smart pull-up on the starting handle brought the engine to immediate life (a good Bugatti engine starts as it stops, instantaneously) and there I was, given the freedom of an admittedly ancient Grand Prix racer and of the extensive Karlskoga paddock. Since this was the only Bugatti I have ever driven, I am grateful for the occasion offering me the car that was more typical of Bugatti design than any other. Of course there was no question of going quickly, but enough opportunity to savour the immediacy of steering feel, the positivity of the brakes, the slickness of the gearbox. Beyond these, everything you may have read about the sweetness of a well-adjusted Bugatti clutch is, I must tell you, perfectly true: lubricated as its faces were by a mixture of oil and kerosene, it enabled this lively racer to be driven easily in conditions where it was sometimes necessary to drop to pedestrian speeds.

One of the pedestrians was a small child, and I deemed it better to steer into what was evidently a cul-de-sac rather than risk the possibility of child and Bugatti crossing paths. That was fine, but then I could not for the life of me remember where reverse gear was to be found. Looking down and around, I saw how near the rear tyre was to my elbow; blessing the narrowness of those primitive tyres, I grasped it and pulled upwards, and found that I was moving the car backwards as effectively as I could desire. It did occur to me that it would have been useful to have had that facility in my old Morgan . . .

The journey to Karlskoga had not been without its moments of interest. I had flown into Göteborg (an atypically handsome town by Swedish standards, it had been laid out by Dutch architects) and there hired one of the new Ford Mustangs that were creating such a marketing furore in the USA. In the course of my journey I found that if one applied the brakes at 100mph one would have completely used them up by the time the speed had dropped to 30mph. Had I been aware of and obedient to the Swedish law which set the maximum rate of road travel at 60mph, I might have made two or three earnest stops before discovering how quickly the Mustang brakes could fade; it just shows how driving fast does save time.

Ford was by no means the only one of the great and famous car makers to upset me by the cynicism they displayed in their business, but they did reveal the taloned foot rather more often, and more disturbingly, than the others. The most serious problem I had with them arose mere months later when, in the course of beating the Firestone drum, I was writing of the importance of equipping a car with tyres that were adequate to their duties. In the course of this I felt obliged to point out that the cheapest version of the Ford Cortina was sold with tyres that, according to the load tables issued by the ETRTO (a tyre trade organization trying to arouse some sense of responsibility and standards), were inadequate to bear at standard pressure the weight of the car even when it was standing still, never mind being up to propelling and manoeuvring it. Shortly afterwards, Setright was on the carpet before his boss. Ford had been calling Firestone to enquire why their PR man was knocking them, and craven Firestone was insisting that I should stop. My boss was insisting that either I should stop or I should go.

It hardly seemed important to me that, after ten months in the PR trade and the discovery that I was not much good at being nice to people I despised, I had no strong ambition to continue. What was much more important was the incompatibility of what was being required of me with my youthful ideals – *magna est veritas et praevalet* ['Truth is great and it prevails'], and all that. At that moment, late in 1966, I elected to become what I have been ever since, an independent writer.

3

COMBATIVE

'Did you really have a death wish?'

The question surprised me. It was asked, a year or two ago, by someone who was on many of the new-car launches to which I used to go, and it apparently reflected the concern felt by several of my colleagues about the pace of my driving.

It was, I felt, an insulting question. Surely anyone of reasonable intelligence could think of some less uncertain, less inconvenient, and very probably less painful way of shuffling off these mortal coils than by provoking a high-speed driving accident? Had I wanted to kick the bucket, I should have studied the subject carefully and found some better way.

The desire to go fast was, as we have noted, already present in that little boy in the back of the Wolseley, back in the slow-moving 1930s. Rather different was

'Long John Kick Start' in the 1960s.

the need to go as fast as possible, for this was a reasoned response to what I considered one of my responsibilities as a motor-noter. It was not enough for me to analyse the engineering and to assess the quality of construction of each car that came to me for review: it was also a moral obligation to describe the dynamic behaviour of the car within the full performance envelope of which it was capable.

Not everybody agreed with me – not even the industry did. When the blanket 70mph speed limit was imposed on Britain in the latter 1960s many a car manufacturer took cynical advantage of it to ignore what might happen beyond, while yet building cars that could indeed venture beyond. The Hillman Avenger, for example, became quite unpleasant beyond 70, although entirely amiable until it reached that speed. It was the same with the component manufacturers: Girling did not require their test drivers to assess their brakes beyond 70, and actually grew quite critical of Bristol who tested them from twice that speed because everything in a Bristol had to work properly at any speed the car could reach. Thus when

Bristol introduced the Avon safety wheel (designed to keep a deflated tyre on the rim) during the currency of the 411 model, the managing director himself (Mr Antony Crook) drove the car at 144mph down a runway at RAF Keeble and, steering with one hand, pressed a switch with the other to detonate a charge which ruptured one of the front tyres. He then braked heavily, threw the car into a slalom which left black marks on the tarmac from all four tyres, came to a halt and pronounced himself satisfied.

That is the spirit. It was a similar conscientiousness that I sought to bring to my own work. I realized that it might come to any driver at some time in his life to feel compelled to drive as fast as possible for some under-standable cause (rushing to an hospital, for instance, or carrying the good news from Aix to Ghent), and if he had bought his car as a result of reading something I wrote about it he was entitled to know what to expect of its behaviour at its limits. My duty was to find out and tell him, before he came unstuck.

My practice was diligent, not to say enthusiastic. In the 1960s the Guild of Motoring Writers (which I joined as soon as I could) ran a test day for British cars at Goodwood, a circuit that I took to with considerable pleasure, very soon finding the best way to negotiate all its corners except perhaps St Mary's, which I always addressed with caution. I remember hammering all sorts of things around there; oddly, the most memorable was by no means one of the fastest or most powerful. It was the little Morgan 4/4, powered (but only just) by a small Ford engine. Out on the circuit its power or lack of it seemed immaterial: the little car simply danced like a *demoiselle* (to call it a Mayfly would not capture its grace) all the way around, taking each bend or corner in a self-generating, self-controlling drift that often angled it a good twenty degrees away from the line of its trajectory yet needed only slight finger pressure on the rim of the steering wheel to monitor and modulate it.

Very few laps were as blissful as those in that little Moggie. I soon reached the conclusion that cars that were good around a racing track were not necessarily good on the road, and *vice versa*, and I still remember as a particularly good example the Austin-Healey

3000, really pleasant as a high-speed touring car but rather befuddled when asked to play racers. I was also having misgivings about the value of racing circuits as test venues, aggravated when the annual test day moved from Goodwood to Silverstone, where there was also a similar day for cars from foreign manufacturers.

Using the old GP circuit at Silverstone (which is the way I like to remember the place – the modern curlicued F1 track is so artificial as to be meaningless), no real issues were likely to emerge below 70mph, but it could be argued that this made it a salutary extension of the law-abiding British motorist's experience. Such was the width of the track that I am not quite convinced by that argument, but the presence of cars and drivers of wildly differing abilities certainly added real-world hazards.

In the course of teaching myself the Silverstone way and becoming (as I had at Goodwood) known as one of the fastest men of the day, I added to my technical repertoire. Noting that many drivers seemed to have trouble with Copse corner, a long right-hander approached at high speed along the pits straight, I worked out a method of exploiting the polar weight shift as the brakes were released. Coming at the corner hard and far over to the left, I braked hard while dropping a gear and allowed the car to develop its full nose-down pitch, often considerable in those days before anti-dive geometry. Sudden release of the brakes caused the front springs to extend and the nose to rise; simultaneously turning into the corner and accelerating hard made the most of all the shifting loads, enabling me to power through the whole corner in a long and satisfyingly stable drift. I learned later to exploit this pitching moment in a variety of difficult circumstances on the road, particularly when a sudden dodge was needed.

It was, realistically enough, on the road that I did the most honing of my technical abilities. People let loose on a racing track have a deplorable tendency to play at being racing drivers, something that I find both embarrassing and frightening. I have no wish to fight someone else for a corner, especially if it be someone to whom I have not been introduced – in which case my ignorance of his driving skills puts me in fear of his very proximity. Motorcycling is an extreme case of this, for many of its accidents arise from contact with another vehicle and the best countermeasure is to stay well away from everybody, even if it means brief resort to some eye-watering acceleration in order to break clear from the menacing pack and away into relatively clear road, where one can perhaps (if only for a while) resume one's chosen pace.

Racing is really rather nasty, as are all competitive sports. Its basis is the desire of chap A to prove himself faster than chap B, but why should that matter to either of them? My concern is to be as good as I can, which is not the same as being as fast as I can but is an absolutely essential prerequisite. If I can do that, it is all that I wish; should I see somebody who is better and faster than I am, I shall be happy to admire him and will endeavour not to obstruct his passage. There is certainly no cause for jealousy: after all, were I among the top one per cent of the motoring population of this country (a not unreasonable ambition), there might accordingly be 200,000 other drivers around who are even better. How nice!

Should anyone feel tempted to object to the idea of top-percentile ranking as 'a not unreasonable ambition', I must admit to a couple of unfair advantages. I take no credit for them, nor any blame for their acquisition: as I have observed elsewhere, the only really clever thing I ever did was to arrange to have exceptional parents, and everything else flowed naturally from that. As well as good peripheral vision I have unusually rapid reflexes. They are easily measured, and many of the systems employed are tolerably accurate. I recall a visit to the Metropolitan Police driving school at Hendon, back in the 1960s, which revealed two quite distinctly different methods of measurement, and after I had broken all records on one of them they took me to the other where I recorded the same result – a little under 0.2 second, which I already knew to be about right. It appears that Stirling Moss had been there before me and clocked 0.2, whereas T C Mits (The Celebrated Man In The Street) and even the man in the police car averages 0.7 second.

Quite honestly, I do not believe that it matters much. All other things being equal it should make a difference, but all other things seldom are equal. What seems to me to matter is not when you react, but how. When something is perceived that demands some reaction, then the brain has to set to work sifting through past instances of a similar nature, cross-checking all the time for minor but possibly significant differences in the circumstances. It may well find nothing, which would be rather a waste of time, so simultaneously other circuits in the grey matter have to run through the problem from known first principles, deducing as the reasoning widens the probable consequences of choosing action A rather than action B. At last an election is made, and only then do we begin to see whether the reaction was correct, or merely promising, or hopelessly wide of the mark.

Do I brake or accelerate? Do I steer right or left? Do I do anything or nothing? Reactions are an idiotic knee-jerk affair; what matters is *judgement*.

To this day I vividly recall a decision to do absolutely nothing. It was taken during the launch of the Citroën CX Turbo, something that Citroën decided to do over the border in Germany where there were some derestricted roads. It was a rainy day, and I was on my own out in the country on a pointlessly meandering B-road that had no camber, no kerbs, poor drainage, and a rather sinister polish to its surface. At some point along one of the curves, going quite fast, I realized that the tyres had very little grip indeed and that the trajectory of the car, if left uncorrected, might well carry its wheels off on to the adjacent greensward which, being likewise wet, would probably provoke all manner of nasty consequences. On the other hand, any attempt to interfere with the present balance of the car in mid-drift could provoke something nastier even sooner. Analysis of the trajectory showed that, if just a trace of speed were lost, it might just tighten enough for all four wheels to stay on the road until it straightened; so, being very careful not to overdo it, I lifted my foot just a shade, and then sat there stock-still, careful to move not a muscle. Two inches from the verge (I should like to have written 2cm, but honesty compels the Imperial measure) the tyres found some grip, restored the car to its intended course, and honour was satisfied.

The occasion was memorable for something else. Citroën had decided to send each of us out driving solo, with no navigator. They wanted to show off a bit about being a firm that was still interested in modern technology, so they had contrived a system which measured distances along our set route and which, at an appropriate point before each corner or navigational hazard, issued suitable instructions through the cassette-player section of the car's radio. Realizing that this put all the day's drivers on an even footing (except, understandably, the French managing director whose car proved, on the fastest bit of Autobahn, to be just that little bit faster than all the others!), I sauntered out afterwards into the *parc fermé* where all the test cars had been put when they returned from the test. I recalled that we had been asked to press a particular button when we crossed the finishing line: that same button had had to be pressed when we started. Could it have operated a timing device? I found a couple of mechanics walking up and down the lines of parked cars (there must have been more than forty) checking figures from each in turn; yes, the cars had been timed. When the mechanics got to the one I had driven there was a marked hiss of air taken in between clenched teeth, and I ventured to ask what results they were finding. When they had finished, they duly reported to me that all the cars had covered the same distance, to within a kilometre or so, during the course of a long morning, but that Setright had been faster *than his nearest rival* by 9 per cent. At last I had the measure of my greater celerity; I kept the knowledge of it to myself, but felt so pleased that all those years of work had not been in vain.

Ave atque vale. 2005.

AFTERWORD

By James May

When I was a teenager, and interested in cars in the way that only teenage boys can be, there were two avenues of enquiry open. One was the populist motoring press; *Autocar*, *Motor*, newspapers and various turgid periodicals about motor mechanics. The other was a rather subversive monthly magazine called *Car*, which was so offbeat that sometimes it didn't even feature a car on its cover.

Most people read the popular stuff, but a few of us, those who wanted something that marked us out as the avant-garde of motoring enthusiasts, chose *Car*. And nothing showed a boy's true mettle quite like leaving *Car* open on any page written by a man called L. J. K. Setright.

Setright was pretty hard going for a fourteen-year-old who hadn't yet considered the significance of Mozart in the development of the car, or who was not fully versed in the works of Horace or Milton, or whose knowledge of the writings of great Jewish scholars was perhaps a bit sketchy. But I stuck with him, even when he lapsed into Latin, and I think it's fair to say Setright helped me learn to write properly, since he did it very well and on a subject I liked. It was that or my O-level text, *The Adventures of Huckleberry Finn*, which remains unopened to this day.

Eventually I ended up in the same business and even, for a while, on the same magazine. So as a young man I observed, slightly baffled, as Setright wavered in his general demeanour and dress sense between 1920s sporting gentleman, Victorian railway magnate and new-age intellectual. The famous beard was the key to a lot of this. By the time I came to know him personally, he and the whiskers had matured into something resembling an Old-Testament prophet and who, to be honest, often sounded like one. It would be wrong to say that Setright towered over those of us who admired him. He preferred to sit in a corner and smoke quietly, available for consultation if anyone dared. 'Do not take notes,' he once almost thundered at me. 'Take responsibility!'

That's not to say there wasn't a lighter side to Setright. Despite his great erudition and wanton bloody-mindedness for the sake of debate, he could resort to a few well-worn catch phrases worthy of any game-show host. Any enquiry into his well-being was always met with, 'So far so good, thank the Lord', unless that enquiry was made at an unacceptable hour (before 10.30) in which case it was, 'A bit too early to tell, really.' He once wrote that, 'Wood is excellent for making trees, but is otherwise not to be trusted.' He also expressed genuine concern that the iniquities of EU regulation would lead to Mozart's *Magic Flute* being renamed *The DIN-standard metal orchestral flute*.

But he could be infuriatingly cussed as well. In his insistence on smoking everywhere and the benefits of doing so, in driving like a lunatic, and in one or two of his less tenable beliefs such as photography got in the way of real journalism. In his celebrated treatise on Bristol Cars, all illustrations were banished to a separate volume, one which the purist was presumably expected to discard.

Setright has been proclaimed a great technical writer, but I think there was more to his writing than that. He was a great writer *per se*, with a wealth of interests to draw on and a style that was at once confrontational and languid as the blue smoke rising from the inevitable Sobranie. But he was technically literate, a man with the mind of an engineering scientist who chose to apply this to his words. He, more than anyone, could cut through the marketing cant and faux science of the motor industry's PR machine to explain exactly why a car felt or worked the way it did (or why it didn't, for that matter). He could instantly distinguish that which was worthy of applause from mere technological tinsel. Whenever I was wrestling with amateur physics in my own writing, it was good to know that Setright was always available for a private seminar on the end of the telephone (or, more often, fax, since it was invariably too early to tell, really). The danger in this was that he might be dissatisfied with what I'd written, and then I'd feel obliged to start again.

Long Lane with Turnings is a suitable testimonial to the man, not least because it finally reveals Setright to be a reassuringly (or is that alarmingly?) normal bloke. He even admits to running and cycling in his youth, which is surprising from one whose idea of exercise was to stand up while smoking.

It has been widely lamented that Setright never finished this work. But I find it strangely apposite. What he did do is, so far, so good. Thank the Lord.

Other Books by L. J. K. Setright

In addition to the books listed below, L. J. K. Setright also wrote regular columns and many extended articles for motoring journals worldwide such as *Car* and *Car & Driver*, engineering design publications, *Punch* and *Penthouse*. He was also the author of religious and musical works. It was in his articles over a period of forty years that his lively and idiosyncratic views engaged people around the world; an article by Setright was once found, together with the Bible, in a rest hut on the higher slopes of K3.